DISCIPLINES OF DELIGHT

DISCIPLINES OF DELIGHT

The Psychoanalysis of Popular Culture

BARRY RICHARDS

FREE ASSOCIATION BOOKS LONDON

First published in 1994 by
Free Association Books Ltd
Omnibus Business Centre
39–41 North Road
London N7 9DP

ISBN 1 85343 325 X

A CIP record for this book is available from
the British Library.

98 97 96 95 94

5   4   3   2   1

Designed, typeset and produced for Free Association Books
by Chase Production Services, Chipping Norton, OX7 5QR
Printed in Finland by WSOY.

CONTENTS

ACKNOWLEDGEMENTS

It will be evident from the Notes indicating the origins of the material in this book (see pp. 163–71) how much it owes to the annual conferences on 'Psychoanalysis and the Public Sphere'. These have been held every autumn at the University of East London since 1987, and are sponsored jointly by the Sociology Department of the University, which in conjunction with the Tavistock Clinic is a major centre for the teaching of psychoanalytic studies in Britain, and by Free Association Books, leading publishers in the psychoanalytic field. When the first of these conferences was held, it was planned as a one-off; it was immediately evident, though, from the interest and enthusiasm aroused, that it should be repeated. Since then, the establishment of psychoanalytic studies in the postgraduate sector in British universities, and the further growth of interest in psychoanalysis in cultural studies and other disciplines, have strengthened the demand for opportunities to explore the interdisciplinary relations of psychoanalysis and to develop contributions from psychoanalytic perspectives to understanding events and processes in the 'public spheres' of culture, politics and society.

The annual UEL/FAB conference has enabled a number of people to develop ideas in a stimulating and supportive context. Four of the chapters of this book had their origins as papers for these conferences, and I am grateful to the people who came to hear them, responded to them and encouraged me to persevere with the line of enquiry which they cumulatively came to represent. Thanks also to Ivan Ward of the Freud Museum, Lawrence Gane and Fred Vermorel of the Royal College of Art, Bob Young and Martin Stanton of the University of Kent for the invitations to present papers at other events, and so for the stimuli to write other material which is incorporated here.

The students comprising the 1993 intake to the MA in Psychoanalytic Studies run jointly by the University of East London and the Tavistock Clinic heard me run through most of the main ideas in the book in a series of classes on 'Psychoanalysis and Popular Culture' as part of that course. They were patient with my preoccupations, heaped on them at the very start of the course, and their comments and questions helped in giving the material its final shape.

A number of people have read or listened to versions of different parts of the book and made helpful comments, or otherwise contributed to the ideas involved in it: John Ballatt, Phil Cohen, Andrew Cooper, Karl Figlio, Christoph Hering, Mica Nava, Clive Perrett, Mike Rustin, Andrew Samuels, Bill Schwarz, Amal Treacher and Alan White. Andrew Blake, Philip Boys, Margaret O'Brien and Lionel Sims have helped make connections. I owe many thanks to the staff, past and present, of Free Association Books, including Ann Scott, Bob Young, who commissioned the book and made many useful comments on a draft manuscript, and Gill Davies. Lastly, thanks to Christoph and Polly for the desk and window, and to Janet and Ruth, with apologies for the absences from everyday life which the study of it seems to involve.

PREFACE

This book has two purposes. Firstly, it is intended as a contribution to two growing areas of academic work. One, already huge, is the study of popular culture and consumption. The other, becoming large but in a patchy and somewhat unintegrated way, is psychoanalytic studies, which includes the use of psychoanalytic ideas in work on society, culture and politics, as well as studies of psychoanalysis from the standpoints of other disciplines. Secondly, it is intended to appeal to readers who are not academic specialists in either of these fields but who are interested in using psychoanalytic ideas to gain more understanding of the contemporary everyday world. It has been written in a way that tries not to presume a familiarity with the theoretical languages which are currently popular in both the cultural studies and psychoanalytic studies fields. Where technical terms are used, an effort has been made to define them as simply as possible.

It is not, the author is all too aware, a work of thorough scholarship. It fails to explore many of the connections to be made with a range of recent works, especially in cultural and social theory. A few connections are noted, but it is left to the reader, or to a future work, to develop these. This book is a collection of essays which illustrate the usefulness of deploying a psychoanalytic sensibility in the interdisciplinary study of society.

The terms of the title, *Disciplines of Delight*, are not used in any technical sense. (Some readers may wish to note that there is no direct influence of the historian Michel Foucault in the choice of the word 'discipline', with which his work is often associated. Though I have found his writings of help in other contexts, the more humanist analysis developed here probably runs counter to Foucault's vision of the modern world.) The meaning of the phrase 'disciplines of delight' is outlined in Chapter 1, and illustrated throughout the book in a number of explorations of everyday experience. At the core of it is the idea that the pleasures of popular culture are at their strongest and best when they confirm us in our sense of belonging to a social order, with all the constraint and disappointment that may involve.

This goes against the grain of some recent 'postmodern' conceptions of pleasure, in which transgression, dissolution or release may be seen at the centre of pleasure. Hopefully there will be enough of interest and plausibility in the detailed observations made about the topics chosen (from the fields of sport, leisure, the motor car, the cigarette and other consumer goods, advertising and popular music) to repay readers who are at odds with the overall argument.

For a book on popular culture this one contains remarkably little material specifically on television and other media. Since it does not purport to be a systematic survey that is not in itself a problem, but it is my hope to address this gap in future work, if not in quite the same mode as here. Also the political implications of the analysis developed here need further examination beyond that given them in Chapter 10.

Barry Richards
April 1994

PART I
INTRODUCTION

1   THE DEPTHS OF THE ORDINARY

VARIETIES OF POPULAR FEELING

What is the emotional appeal of the major forms of popular culture? Are there common psychological themes to be found in apparently diverse areas of everyday life? To what extent is our 'mass culture' of leisure and entertainment one of manipulation and shallowness, or one of choice and contentment? What can we learn about ourselves and our social world through the study of mundane forms of enjoyment?

This book offers a discussion of these questions, and some answers to them, in a way that is intended to be of interest both to the 'general reader', if such a worthy type still exists, and to the academic student of contemporary society and cultural change. It is deliberately selective, one-sided and relatively short, on the assumption that its argument has a better chance of impressing itself upon a broad range of readers if it is borne along by some vivid examples, rather than being carried within an intricate apparatus of theory. (Moreover the development of theories of relevance to the understanding of popular culture, stemming from work in social history, anthropology, ethnography, semiotics, women's studies, and elsewhere, has proceeded at an alarming pace in recent years, and this author is in no position to attend to many of them adequately.) At the same time this book will hopefully provide some satisfying concepts for readers with an appetite for theory, although the 'general theory of popular culture' with which it apparently grandly begins is, to say the least, rudimentary.

Whether passionate or casual, positive or negative, our relationships to the phenomena of mass culture such as music, sport and consumer goods are important both in our daily lives and in the task of understanding contemporary society. As any thoughtful observation suggests, and the

now extensive literature of cultural studies shows, we encounter in popular culture a rich particularity, that is,
different kinds of processes at work in different situations.
The rise of the television chat show, the growth of various
forms of counselling, the spread of hypermarkets and the
appearance of regular car boot sales are linked in that they
have all resulted in familiar components of the present-day
life worlds of millions, but it would be a rash observer who
judged them to express a single underlying socio-historical
process.[1] People have diverse and often contradictory needs
and aspirations, and much of the prevalent wisdom in
academic studies of society is to stress difference and
diversity.

However, while acknowledging the fundamental importance of a close attention to the particular processes involved in different contexts, the concern of this book is to
establish a recurrent theme in everyday culture. This concern is to some extent at odds with much recent work
which has pointed to the dissolution and fragmentation of
popular culture, and has suggested that the old mass forms
have largely given way to a highly segmented or pluralistic,
'postmodern', scenario. Here, people (though still grouped
into cultural fractions) are seen as pursuing a range of quite
different agendas, unconstrained by any 'grand narrative' of
history or community.

Just as the monolithic industrial forms of employment in
mill, mine, factory and so on have given way to a fluid job
market with new divisions of labour in a multiplicity of
changing service industries, and to the emptiness of unem-
ployment, so have the uniform patterns of release in the
pubs, football grounds and seaside resorts given way to a
shifting profusion of pleasures. These include, for example,
the multi-coloured subcultural sparks showering from the
volcano of a once homogeneous 'youth culture'. If it had
ever been possible to map youthful identities onto a simple
mod versus rocker battlefield, no ready reckoner of style
could now be devised, as the ethnic and class recomposition
of Britain and changes in sexual vocabulary have lent weight
to the creative impulses towards diversity (and the commercial pressures towards niche marketing). Similarly, and notwithstanding the standardising effects of the concentration
of retailing in the hands of relatively few major players, the
variety of possible expressions of adult, domestic taste in

design, food and clothing is far too great for any ordinary consumer to be familiar with all the nuances.

Central to this process of differentiation are of course the media, most obviously the specialist magazines, the narrowcasting radio stations and about-to-proliferate TV channels, which both in their advertising material and in their editorial/programme content are intensively engaged in the constant elaboration of their audiences' identities. Whether knowingly party to this project or not, we are all bound to some degree into the work of identifying ourselves as different from others in our leisure and consumption choices.

The main idea of this book has to be set in the context of this current awareness of difference, to which it is intended as a complement rather than a corrective. It will be argued here that some of the key forms of popular culture deal with tensions which are universal in the modern world. Not only is it possible to apprehend some of the most important meanings of cultural forms, but we can postulate these to be widely shared. This argument will be based on a predominantly *psychological* examination of the meanings of these particular types of cultural practice or product. A consideration of the psychic dimensions of cultural participation suggests that – both in the present and the foreseeable future – popular culture will continue in at least some sectors to be a 'mass' culture, because it can provide helpful ways of managing internal anxieties and conflicts from which we all suffer.

It will also be observed that, just as the 'masses' are alive and well, so also the typical 'elite' reaction to mass culture – dismissal and contempt – is still a key feature of the cultural landscape, as we might expect from John Carey's (1992) anatomising of the virulent elitism at the centre of British intellectual life in recent times. Taking our cues from this centre we British, in school and elsewhere, all learn to scorn the popular, or at best to treat our love for popular cultural forms with amused condescension. In this context, another purpose of this book is to defend some forms of mass culture, in terms that (being largely psychological) will be a combination of the moral and the aesthetic. That which is popular can be, indeed may often be, profound; some durable values may inhabit our uses of the cheap, commercial and ephemeral. Among the ordinary enjoyments of life we may encounter the deepest questions, if not some answers.

AGENCY AND PLEASURE

Of course the definition of 'popular culture' is problematic
(see, for example, Nowell-Smith, 1987). Both words in this
term have rich yet uncertain meanings, and raise many
conceptual problems (see Williams, 1983). To circumvent
these, the term will be taken here to refer loosely and simply
to any practices and experiences which involve at least large
minorities of the population in any national culture, and for
access to which no socially restricted qualification (in terms of
education, wealth or social networks) is required.[2]

The conceptual difficulties need not stand in the way of
an attempt here to formulate a rough, general theory of
popular culture. This rests on three axioms. Firstly, our
participation in popular culture is basically as voluntary
agents. We are not the helpless manipulatees of an all-
powerful 'culture industry', as some versions of critical social
theory have implied, nor the passive recipients of a monolithic 'socialisation', as some varieties of psychology have
suggested. Research findings, everyday observation and recent work in cultural theory all converge on the understanding that important capacities for discrimination and choice
are exercised in many areas of mass cultural experience.
This is not to say that we must assume, in neo-liberal
fashion, that an inalienable right to choose is *always* being
exercised, even in the most banalised or damaging forms of
experience. Nor is it to overlook the fact that the notion of
agency is, at many levels, a difficult one. But in an
important sense we are active, and often creative, in our
reception and use of the artefacts and experiences offered
by popular culture.

Secondly, we derive satisfaction from participation in
popular cultural forms; if we did not, we would not
participate in them and they would not be popular. To say
this much is to assume some loosely utilitarian basis to
human conduct; it is to assume that we would not persist,
en masse and voluntarily, in experiences that brought no
satisfaction. It does not, however, entail assuming that any
such satisfaction is complete and without its own contradictions.[3]

Thirdly, the pleasures we obtain from participation in
popular cultural forms derive from two sources. The first is

in the libidinal, sensual satisfactions which may be available – the physical pleasures of sport, the regressive delights of absorption in music, and so on. The second is in the reassurances and satisfactions brought by the essentially social nature of popular cultural activity, however reclusive some of its forms may be. Participation in popular culture reaffirms the containing social matrix of which we are a part, to which we belong and which belongs to us.

It is to this third point – the complex psychological nature of the satisfactions to be obtained in popular culture – that most of this book addresses itself. In doing so it draws heavily upon psychoanalytic theory, or rather upon a particular reading of psychoanalytic theory. The previous paragraph is in part a restatement of the Freudian concept of 'sublimation', the idea that our need for pleasure can be deflected into socially valuable activities. Freud theorised that sexual pleasures could be substituted by non-sexual ones, and more generally that bodily pleasures could be substituted by non-bodily ones. This idea will be taken up on occasions in the following chapters, though rather than simply applying the concept of sublimation to popular culture, we will be looking at the greater depth and texture which can be added to this and other classical Freudian concepts if we revisit them through the thinking of some post-Freudian traditions.

We will consider the understandings of sublimation which are possible in the light of the Kleinian and object-relations traditions of psychoanalytic work. We will see how Klein's concept of 'reparation' – the idea that we need to feel we are doing some good things in life to help us live with the guilt we all feel about our destructive feelings – both overlaps with and extends the concept of sublimation.

DELIGHT IN DISCIPLINE

From this interdependence of people arises an order *sui generis*, an order more compelling and stronger than the will and reason of individual people composing it. (p. 230)

The individual is compelled to regulate his conduct in an increasingly differentiated, more even and more stable manner. (p. 232)

The coexistence of people, the intertwining of their inten-
tions and plans, the bonds they place on each other, all
these, far from destroying individuality, provide the medium
in which it can develop. (p.356)

(Norbert Elias, *The Civilising Process*, Vol. 2)

It will be argued that the sensual component (the libidinal,
as Freud called it) is often preserved in the cultural
experience, and sometimes in quite undeflected form, but
that it is held within a framework which is essentially one
of constraint. It is only within frameworks of social constraint – that is, of relationships to other individuals and to
images of wider communities – that we can become individuals, capable of agency and responsibility. Adherence to
such a framework bestows pleasures which are not derived
from sublimated libido but exist in themselves, in the
satisfactions of autonomy, maturity and the exercise of
developmental capacities. The social discipline is both a
container for pleasurable experience originating fundamentally in the body, and is also a source of delight in itself. In
this way, in the struggle between reality and pleasure which
Freud (1911) saw as being central to psychological development, the reality principle can *subsume* the pleasure principle
– it does not just contradict it.

In a sense, perhaps, it is because culture allows us spaces
in which we can find pleasure that we are so deeply attached
to it. We love the boundaries as much as the spaces, since the
two are inseparable. We need to share meanings and to
engage in activities with others, to partake of the disciplines
of sociality, in order to be able to take the pleasures of
sensuality. And those disciplines themselves are also saturated
with sensual delight through their having been constructed in
the early years of development, when bodily experience and
cultural experience are fused. We learn our first lessons about
social limits and personal responsibilities in relationships
which are intensely sensual.

But our love of, and delight in, the powers which constrain
us is probably best thought of, at the most basic level, in
terms of the gratitude which, if fortunate enough, we can feel
towards our begetters. This is immediately felt in relation to
the parents who produced and nurtured us, and then ex-

tended symbolically to social authorities, though it is also realistically due to the society which provides (or rather, *is* the provision of) some experience of community, however attenuated or disrupted that may be. Gratitude may be due for being the individual one is, with whatever hopes and resources, but is also for being one among others, for the experience of belonging.

To sum up, we could say that this book will therefore explore in some specific contexts the ways in which cultural experience is fundamentally sensual, and in which bodily and material pleasures are fundamentally social. It will do so in a way that presents a basically appreciative, psychoanalytically-informed analysis of popular culture.

PSYCHOANALYSIS AND TAKING SIDES

There is no established psychoanalytic perspective on popular culture. However, it would probably not be difficult to piece together, from the psychoanalytic literature, some kind of appraisal of popular culture, and it would probably be a negative one.[4] Many of the most commonly consumed products in the fields of popular literature, cinema, television and video can be seen as at best sentimental and at worst perverse, in the technical senses of being unable to tolerate reality (Chasseguet-Smirgel, 1985) or of expressing hatred and destructiveness (Hinshelwood, 1989; Hering, 1994). We could find many psychoanalytic grounds for subscribing to the view that popular culture is often the enemy of psychic truth, in its preferences for simplicity, entertainment and evasion over the complex and painful.

This view – if then generalised to the whole field of popular culture – would be consistent with a particular kind of class experience: that of the educated and, in the traditional sense of the word, 'cultured' middle and upper classes, for whom the high culture of literature, the visual arts and classical music is the primary mode of aesthetic experience, and a major expression of moral value. This kind of class-based orientation is the 'default' position of psychoanalysis – that is to say, unless its attention is deliberately refocused elsewhere, then the psychoanalytic contribution to the study of culture will tend to reproduce the terms of this world view and its spontaneous orientation towards high culture. This is because, despite its many sympathies with radical causes and its own marginality in relation to the establishment, the culture of psychoanalysis is still, loosely speaking, an upper middle class one. (This is certainly so in the British context, though the same could probably be said of most other countries where psychoanalysis has become established.) This is the stratum from which many of its patients and practitioners come. It is also the culture which (albeit perhaps in ambivalent ways) has historically nurtured psychoanalysis in a generally hostile environment, as the relationship of analysis to the Bloomsbury group in the inter-war years illustrates. (Freud was translated and published by this most conspicuous of intellectual elites.)

For the majority, though, this kind of cultural orientation is not spontaneous, nor helpful in making sense of their biographical and day-to-day experience. For those legions of us born into working and lower middle class cultures the stuff of aesthetic life is more likely to be found in things like television, both in its content and in its form as a medium, in other forms of mass entertainment and leisure, in the urban and suburban landscapes we inhabit, in the objects we buy or covet, in advertising and commercial design, and in popular music. Whatever later exposures we might have had to theatres and orchestras, painters and poets, our aesthetic commitments were shaped elsewhere, by the sounds of Radio Luxemburg (or its more diversified successors in pop music radio) rather than those of the Third Programme, as the BBC classical music station used to be called, by the shapes and colours of consumer goods rather than by the conventional icons of 'art', and by *Coronation Street* and other television soaps rather than Shakespeare.

The social sciences were once, like psychoanalysis is still, predominantly given to the pursuit of questions and concerns defined by the class experience of the elite strata. However, with the extension of higher education and of the social sciences in the 1960s, this position changed in ways with which we are now very familiar. Dispossessed and sometimes angry voices from the lower strata came to be heard, and in some areas of work have come to predominate in the shaping of research problematics and theoretical paradigms. This has been a mixed development, though on balance a strongly positive one. It has brought new energy and a concern with social justice to some areas of work which would otherwise have been elitist and complacent. It has opened up new avenues of research and brought new illumination to old problems, though it has also brought new kinds of dogma and complacency.

Readers with cultural studies or sociological backgrounds will not need to be told that a very well known example of this development was the programme of work undertaken by the Centre for Contemporary Cultural Studies at the University of Birmingham in the 1970s, in which a group of young sociologists of predominantly working and lower middle class backgrounds set about the sociological and historiographical discovery of the popular cultures in which they had grown up. Through their influence, 'youth subcultures' became a favoured research topic (see, e.g., Hall and Jefferson, 1976). Theirs was a basically appreciative stance; the inventiveness and subtlety of popular culture was stressed. There was also a neo-Marxist celebration of the oppositional quality of popular cultural forms, in their subversive appropriations of elements of bourgeois, commodified or official culture, and their resistance to the disciplines of the workplace, market and state. This assumption that popular culture is intrinsically pitted against a dominant order, or that it has the dynamics of class conflict at its heart, has been set aside in the development of this field of work towards more complex – and in some ways, postmodern – problematics. It has also become clear that the distinctions between popular and high or elite culture are no longer central to a map of cultural differences and tensions (see e.g., MacCabe, 1986, and Willis, 1990). Yet in the wider culture much debate about the merits of the popular is still dominated by the elite canon.

In the emergence of cultural studies, though, there was a much needed recognition and exploration of the importance of popular culture as a central topic for social research and as the major medium in which, and resource with which, most people live their lives. In the subsequent development of cultural theory there has also been an understanding that *tensions* of one sort or another are fundamental to the production and consumption of popular culture, though these tensions can be characterised in various ways: hegemonic versus counter-hegemonic, rational versus irrational, global versus local, and so on.

This book will propose something equivalent in the psycho-

analytic approach to aesthetics – to turn it towards a sympathetic analysis of popular culture, and to base that analysis on
a particular characterisation of the central tension – one in
which its 'disciplining' force will be seen not as set against its
democratic and life-enhancing functions, but as intrinsic to
them. This will be done with reference to particular sectors of
popular culture, and two points need to made about the
implications – especially the political implications, in the wide
sense of 'politics' – of the book's chosen terrain.

The first is that the overall tone may seem to be unduly
positive, too appreciative of the merits of popular culture and
neglectful of its more alienated or destructive aspects. If
critique is an essential ingredient of any piece of social
analysis, this is a failing, but the view taken here is that in
the context of the still prevalent elitism a degree of partisan
one-sidedness is an appropriate contribution, rather like the
emphasis on the unifying aspect of popular culture referred to
above. None the less, the aim has not been to present a
relentlessly up-beat view of the topics considered, and I hope
to have registered the ambivalence that culture reflects, and
the limits of particular forms of it as resources for emotional
development.

It will be clear, though, that many of the phenomena under
study are discussed as valuable social institutions. This is not
because – as much cultural studies work has seen it – popular
culture is a form of *resistance* against an oppressive hegemonic
culture (though it may sometimes and importantly be that),
but because it is a rich and powerful form of modern human
community.

Secondly, it will be obvious that a number of the cultural
forms to be examined are quite strongly gendered in their
historical development and their range of contemporary
meanings, in that they are sites of predominantly male
participation. While all writing about society may to some
extent be autobiographical, and driven by the personal
interests of the writer, the selection of some of the topics
to be dealt with here was defined quite closely by the
author's own experience, as a man in a particular social
location. This is regrettable to the extent that some female
readers may be less likely to take up the book, but is
defensible on the grounds that the structures of feeling
which can be discerned underlying these stereotypically
masculine interests are in fact universal. Any window onto

these structures is bound to be from a particular vantage point (see also Chapter 8, p. 129), but once identified they can be appreciated from other such points at different social locations, from within different biographies and different cultural forms. The aim here is also to discuss their specificities in ways that will enable readers who do not share these enthusiasms to find something of interest in the accounts of them, along the route to the more general conclusions.

The result is, hopefully, a thoroughly psychosocial study, which explores the psychic meanings and emotional resonances of some key cultural phenomena while also attending to their historical and political dimensions. Not least here is the triad of variables now often taken to be the central concerns of social science. *Class* provides the animating spirit for the whole book, not in a Marxist fashion but in a concern with the persistent reverberations which the traditional class structure continues to have in many domains of culture, even though that structure has now been substantially modified at the economic level. *Gender*, as just noted, has guided the selection of topics, though it will be argued that this does not entail a gendering of the whole analysis. *Race* is present throughout the book, and arguably much depends on the extent to which cultural forms such as those described here can contain the difficulties in dealing with ethnic difference which are the major potential source of hatred and violence in many contemporary societies.

2 WHAT IS THE PSYCHO-ANALYTIC STUDY OF CULTURE?

This second introductory chapter will consider some of the issues involved in the use of psychoanalytic theory as an instrument of cultural analysis.[1] As a methodology chapter, it could be skipped by readers not particularly interested in abstract questions of method, or returned to after some or all of the case studies in Part II have been read, in the course of which some questions may be raised in readers' minds about what kind of study this is. It will try to clarify what kind of activity we are engaged in when we use psychoanalytic concepts to assist us in the exploration and study of social and cultural processes. We will consider a number of possible paradigms or names for this activity.

RESEARCH

Sometimes (e.g. Dahmer, 1993) the term 'research' is used in this connection. But much of the psychoanalytically informed writing about contemporary culture does not contain work which could be called 'research' in the conventional social-scientific senses of the word. It is important to note that these include not only 'number crunching', statistical researches of the kind represented in some well known traditions of sociological research, nor just the model of experimental research which has dominated psychology for much of its history. The array of research methods now widely regarded as mainstream in the social and human sciences is much wider than is sometimes assumed. There are many qualitative methods of some depth and subtlety, based on the analysis of various kinds of textual material, observational data and interview transcripts. Some of these methods have concerns in common with clinical therapeutic work, for example, there is a long history of using biographical and autobiographical material, and this is becoming more popular among some social researchers (see, e.g., Bertaux, 1981; Denzin, 1989; Rosenthal, 1990; Lunt and Livingstone, 1992).

What is normally taken to be the hallmark of a research method is its *systematic* nature. This is normally expected at two levels, firstly in the sampling and secondly in the analysis. On the first count, it is expected that the sample of people, texts or whatever is being studied has been derived in some systematic way, according to defensible criteria. In some research in progress on advertising and its psychosocial significance, for example, we have to decide on looking at ads for particular products in particular media at particular times, and we have to justify these choices in relation to our research objectives.

As well as systematic sampling, there has to be systematic analysis. This is to say that an explicit set of procedures must be followed consistently in the analysis of the material. For example, social scientists have put a lot of effort into developing coding methods for analysing qualitative data. Such methods can enable us to take, say, many thousands of advertisements and work out a way of identifying the major themes to be found in all or a number of them, or of differentiating them into subgroups according to their major preoccupations, or of assessing the extent to which they provide evidence in support of any hypothesis about advertising content. Thus some Canadian researchers have shown that during the course of this century print advertising has shifted towards an increasing use of magical rather than rational strategies – that is, products are presented more in terms of the magical transformations they effect upon the consumer than in terms of their actual characteristics and functions (Leiss *et al*, 1990). This conclusion, of some value to the understanding of modern culture, is dependent upon the application of coding procedures to a systematic sample.

Although much social research of this sort produces data and conclusions which may be of great psychoanalytic interest, not much of the explicitly psychoanalytic work on culture has had the quality of systematicity in either sampling or analysis, let alone in both. One leading example of work in this field is the writing of the American historian Christopher Lasch, two of whose books (1978; 1984) have been considered – rightly – among the most influential recent works in the psychoanalytic study of culture. Lasch argued that certain social and cultural developments in modern society have weakened our capacities for working through the processes of psychological separation, and have rendered people more prone to seek regressive solutions to the pains of life. His books range over vast cultural territories: changes in family life; education, sport and gender relations; cinema, literature and art; cold war mentalities and nuclear survivalism; images of ageing and the old; and so on. Lacking any systematic empirical method, and referring only to examples drawn mainly from the press and other writings which illustrate the overall argument, these works are vulnerable to the attacks which have been made on them for their alleged cultural 'conservatism' (e.g. Barrett and McIntosh, 1982; their's and other critiques are dicussed in Richards, 1985b). Arguably, the many insights Lasch offered have been less well received than they might otherwise have been because of this. Certainly if we want to take an appreciative view of his work then we have to see it as something other than 'research'.

The same can be said of the writings of Paul Hoggett (1992), which like those of Lasch are organised firmly around a rhetorical objective but which encompass references to and discussions of a very wide range of materials – literary, everyday, philosophical, political – linked by their place in the author's argument but not by their locations in space and time.

Sometimes in the now quite large body of recent work in this field the makings of a systematic method can be discerned. At the core of an essay by Karl Figlio (1989), for example, on unconscious aspects of the politics of health, is an attempt to take a series of key words and to explore their conscious and unconscious meanings. Figlio shows how some words in ideological discourse (like 'nation' or 'nature') easily become the vehicles for crude psychic defences, while words such as 'public' carry with them more benign emotional freight – less evocative, but no less profound. A full-scale historical study of the usage of words (on the lines of Raymond Williams' *Keywords*) may provide confirmatory evidence of such arguments, but that would be a very large undertaking. In Figlio's paper it is the author's associations to the words on which the analysis primarily rests.

This draws attention to a major problem in the psychoanalytic study of society: the danger that our conclusions may be highly projective, deriving from the student's internal world rather than accurately reflecting the external society. This echoes the frequent criticism of psychoanalytic therapy that the therapist's interpretations are subjective and unconfirmed. The psychoanalytic clinician can reply that the disciplines and the data of the clinical setting can overcome this problem, but as observers at large in society we have no such rationale. If – as is the case here – we choose not to adopt the systematic method required of research, and so cannot construct our enterprise in those terms, then we have to look for some other conceptualisation of what we are doing to legitimate it.

THEORY

Another solution might be to define one's work as theory, which gives a very wide freedom to engage with what one wants to. Much of the interest in psychoanalysis in cultural studies has been set in this mode. But theory too has to be systematic. The present work also falls short of some of the requirements of good theoretical work, in that it does not include efforts to engage systematically with other sets of ideas of relevance to its field. The reader may notice a certain patchiness in the extent to which this is done; it tends to occur in places where references to others' ideas were helpful to the analysis, or easily appended. There are no doubt many omissions which would be embarrassing if it were understood by readers that the book purported to be a piece of full-blooded theory. There is a theory of sorts on offer here, as indicated in Chapter 1, in the sense of a core idea elaborated in various contexts, but not in the sense of a rigorously defined set of propositions distinguished from other theories.

Theorists are obliged to consult the evidence, but not to produce any, and in the realms of social and cultural theory are anyway given considerable licence to spend a lot of their energies engaging with other theorists. In another context we might want to defend the virtues of theoretical work, but here the main point is that in much of the work which has been concerned with how psychoanalytic approaches might inform the study of popular culture, and indeed of society as a whole, the preference has been for theoretical debate rather than systematic empirical study. This might be all right for a while, but of course in the longer run it has to connect with something empirical if it is to command much respect.

Where empirical material has been used it is often in a highly selective way, as in writings on particular films, advertisements, television programmes, and so on, chosen for their interest to the writer. This returns us to the problem of whether such work – and indeed the case studies in this book – can be called 'research'.

CLINICAL ANALOGIES

It may be thought that this problem is an unnecessary one, and that we should not want to legitimate psychoanalytic work by the standards of 'research'. Perhaps it would be more appropriate to take as our model not social science but psychoanalysis itself in its original clinical form, and to see the psychoanalytic study of culture as an analogous form of analysis. Freud after all saw therapy as research, and while the equivalence does not hold if we invert it, we may still be able best to conceptualise the nature of our 'research' in the terms of clinical practice. Clinical analysis and cultural analysis seem to share a number of features. Both are concerned with exploring the unconscious meanings of the everyday, and indeed analytic work going on daily in sessions all over the world may be constantly generating insights into everyday culture which are not captured in intellectual work, unless either analyst or analysand writes them up for publication.

Secondly, the style of psychoanalytic investigation which will be described here is based in part on the use of experience, in the form of reflection on one's individual feelings about and responses to particular phenomena. At times it will appear to be dealing with an individual's 'associations', that is to thoughts which freely enter the mind in connection with the phenomenon in question. This kind of working over and conceptualising of experience and associations is also a key component of the therapeutic process.

There are however some obvious and major differences. For the clinician, the object of interpretations and the audience for those interpretations are one and the same, the patient. The cultural analyst's audience may not experience themselves as the object of the analysis. On the other hand, therapeutic analysis is concerned with the experience of a person other than the analyst, a fact which is modified but not fundamentally altered by the more recent emphasis in analysis on counter-transference.

This term refers to ways in which the *analyst's* experience is unconsciously influenced by the patient's states of mind and ways of relating; most present-day analysts regard it as an important source of information about the *patient*. It supplements the older idea of transference, in which the patient experiences the analyst in ways determined by deeply buried feelings, expectations and fears rather than by the reality of the analyst's presence. The understanding of the transference is the key to understanding the patient in classical psychoanalysis; for some present-day analysts, the key is to be found in the counter-transference.[2]

In the mode of cultural analysis which follows in this book, the analyst is also the patient, the source of material (sometimes in the direct sense of producing it, by generating associations to cultural phenomena, more often in the indirect sense of collecting and presenting material from various sources). The possibilities for reality-testing which may be available in the consulting room are therefore not to hand; while the analyst may help the patient to disentangle reality from phantasy, no such help is available to the student of culture. The screen the researcher faces is not an analyst with a capacity to comment on the thoughts one is having, but the everyday world of images and artefacts which cannot answer back to one's projections, and there is a clear risk that the researcher's observations may say more about the researcher than about the object of study.

Nonetheless, it has recently been suggested by Andrew Samuels (1993) that the cultural analyst strives to get into a transference–counter-transference relationship to the cultural problem under investigation, trying to understand it in terms of its antecedents (i.e. its history, and the meanings attached to it) and to raise the level of the culture's consciousness of it to allow some knowledge of and control over the problem. This is to see the work of cultural study as directly analogous to therapeutic work, where the therapist tries to bring to the patient some insight into the problem, partly by using the evidence of the counter-transference as to the nature of the patient's feelings. As Figlio (1993) points out, pursuing the therapeutic model in this way raises the awkward question of whether, prior to the analyst's 'counter-transference' towards culture, that culture has a 'transference' to the analyst. This is an awkward question because it is not clear what meaning this term can have if it is applied to something other than an individual human subject and agent. 'Culture' is not a subject who has walked into a consulting room. As Jenny Shaw (1994) has shown, in a particular research context (the Mass Observation Archive), subjects or respondents may show a powerful transference to the social researcher, but this is not the same as 'culture' forming a transference: it is difficult to specify what this might mean.

Moreover the objects of analysis in the present work are not for the most part 'problems', and so a therapeutic strategy would be inappropriate here. (Chapter 10 returns to this question of the usefulness of a diagnostic approach to culture.) So while we might agree with Samuels that the emotional and even bodily reactions of the analyst can be as important in understanding culture as counter-transference may be in understanding the patient (and there will be some examples of this in later chapters), a fully analogous, let alone homologous, relationship between the two activities does not seem to hold.[3]

CRITICISM

Overall, then, whatever parallels there may sometimes be between clinical practice and psychoanalytic studies of culture, we have to find an independent conceptualisation of the latter, or to link it with some other more appropriate practice. As another possibility we can turn to the fairly well-established modes of psychoanalytic literary criticism. Here the problem of the choice of material, to which the researcher responds with systematicity, is resolved by the identification of traditions and genres and by the choice of specific texts, and the analysis is guided by some systematic principles. There has been a lot of controversy about what those principles can or should be – about whether it is the author, the characters, the text or the reader that is the focus of inquiry – but at least there are some principles which can be appealed to or argued over. The Rustins' (1987) work, for example, demonstrates that the psychological meanings of children's fiction, and the part it can play in emotional development, can be illuminated by the consistent application of a particular psychoanalytic approach to the narrative content.

In some contexts, then, it may be possible to co-opt psychoanalytic investigations into an established field of practice – here, literary criticism – as an approach to compare and perhaps contend with others, and so gain for them a certain legitimacy. A strong version of this position (see e.g. Peter Brooks, 1987) would suggest that psychoanalysis should have a privileged status in literary analysis, because of the particular light it can throw on the text (in Brooks' version, on the meanings of literary forms). There is also in Brooks' concept of criticism a parallel to Samuels' conception of culture-as-patient – a similarly problematic notion that the text is, somehow, the analysand.

Nevertheless, in what has been said here, there is in fact a basis for the co-option of the kind of psychoanalytic work in the following chapters into the project of criticism. In referring to the example of psychoanalytic literary criticism, and in making the point that psychoanalytic explorations of culture can utilise the explorer's own experience, we are implicitly talking about a *sensibility* and its use. That is to say, one way to think of psychoanalytic work in the fields of popular culture, everyday life and politics is as the exercise of a sensibility.

Given the long and complex history of the term 'sensibility', its introduction here may create more problems than it solves. It has at least two current meanings. In one, it is an especially acute sensitivity – as *The Concise Oxford Dictionary* puts it, an 'exceptional openness to emotional impressions'. In the other, which we shall use here, it is the *capacity* to feel – and in this context, the psychoanalytic sensibility means the capacity to feel in a certain kind of way, distinct from and perhaps complementary to other ways. Psychoanalysis can be understood as a particular form of sensibility. Its substantive specificity lies in the significance placed upon certain kinds of feelings such as loss, guilt, reparation and rivalry. It has no necessarily privileged access to such feelings, but its consistent use will make it more likely that they will be attended to in a sustained and subtle way. Psychoanalysis has, or indeed is, a rich vocabulary for the articulation of such feelings, especially insofar as they are normally subliminally hidden.

So as a tradition of thinking about feeling, and indeed as a way of accessing feelings, psychoanalysis can be seen as the basis for a sensibility which can be deployed in a number of different fields. As a consequence, certain key dimensions of human experience and action – the ubiquity of conflict, anxiety, desire and omnipotence – are likely to be focused on, whatever the empirical field of study.

Thus we can arrive at a general conception of the psycho-analytic study of culture and society as a kind of criticism, if that is understood as the deployment of a sensibility, or tradition of feeling. Also, we might see criticism as typically being concerned to locate its object in frameworks of meaning. This certainly happens in psychoanalytic studies, where things are *interpreted*. As we have seen, though, the interpretations are of a different order from those made by the clinician, since they are not made within the context of the very particular kind of personal relationship which is the basis of clinical work.

Moreover, the role of the critic can be said to involve not only the exercise of a particular sensibility but its location or contextualisation in relation to other sensibilities; or, to put it differently, the generation of some 'interdiscursive' reflections. Similarly, it is the responsibility of any psychoanalytic study of non-clinical phenomena to address the various disciplinary and empirical contexts within which those phenomena need to be located if we are to understand them in a sufficiently complex way. This is particularly difficult in the case of popular culture, where we confront an endless sprawl of potentially interesting phenomena, around which all the disci-plines of the social sciences and the humanities can and increasingly do play.

In such a field it becomes clear that the role we are trying to fashion is even more uncomfortably broad than those of literary, art and film critics. It is probably best described as that of 'social critic', or purveyor of 'cultural criticism'. There is no agreed job specification for the post of 'social/cultural critic', and there can easily be a smell of grandiosity about the idea of one.[4] Despite these problems, the appellation of 'critic' is frequently used today in blurbs and credits. However loose, arrogant and faddish though it may in some contexts be, the notion of 'cultural criticism' may be of some use as a provisional characterisation of what is being attempted in the following chapters. It indicates the rationale for the method, namely that it should be understood as the application of a certain kind of sensibility. This sensibility is characterised by a preoccupation with certain kinds of feelings and with their non-obviousness in everyday life, by an interpretive method based on associations, and by an awareness of (and where possible an attempt to engage with) the social contexts – historical, political, economic, and so on – which lie outside its interpretive scope.

In opting for this conceptualisation of the following essays we are not necessarily giving up on the project of psychoanalytically-informed research as a more systematic study of a more circumscribed object; that is something else.[5] Also, as Helmut Dahmer (1993) describes, forms of research are possible in which psychoanalytic techniques contribute in a basic way to the generation of data rather than just to its analysis, as in the work of the European 'ethno-psychoanalysts' and their interviewing techniques (and also, in a usually less sophisticated but very extensive way, in the small-group and interview research done commercially for decades by some market researchers).

Nor are we abandoning the aim of a psychoanalytic contribution to social theory; that, however, needs to be linked to systematic research. Hopefully its development can be stimulated by the kind of criticism illlustrated here.

After this broad outline of what is being undertaken in the following 'case studies', we can now turn to the first of them. The order in which they appear is not particularly significant, being that which seemed best suited to the exposition of the main recurrent theme. Readers who wish to read some but not others, or to take them in a different order, will not be seriously inconvenienced, though some references in the text may assume their order as presented.

PART II
CASE STUDIES

3   THE GLORY OF THE GAME

THE PASSION FOR FOOTBALL

The first example[1] which will be taken to develop the method
and the theoretical approach described in Chapters 1 and 2 is
that of association football, or soccer as it has been called,
from 'soc' – appropriately so (for reasons to be given in this
chapter), though the term has become less frequent in Britain
recently. Some basic Freudian concepts can be seen to be
very useful in understanding the psychology of the game, in a
way that also points towards the need for other, more
post-Freudian thinking as well.

A passion for football is part of the fabric of life for
many of us, especially if we are or have been boys. Of all
the case studies to be considered, this is perhaps the most
'gender-biased', though the explanation for this is not entirely self-evident. There are no obvious, intrinsic reasons
why football should not appeal as much to, and involve as
many, women as it does men. However, for whatever
complex and deep historical reasons, we have a situation in
which the popular imagination is mobilised around the sight
of *men* in sporting action far more readily and powerfully
than around that of women. Of the mass spectator sports,
only tennis and athletics seem to generate images of women
participants as famous and compelling as those of men –
images of athleticism, endurance and skill. Hopefully we are
dealing here with a contingent effect which gradually increasing rates of female participation in other sports will
change, rather than with an enduring mystique of the male
body as a necessarily privileged signifier of strength, commitment, painful effort, virtuosity and all the other heroic
values which we seek in sport.

The passion for football, gendered to a great extent as it
may currently be, needs to be understood at two levels.
Firstly it must be seen as a passion of partisanship, involving
the expression of local and national patriotisms and other

forms of partisan attachment. Secondly, we must ask why
football, more than any other sport, has become the vehicle
for passions of this partisan sort. Why, at first in Britain and
then very rapidly in many other countries, did the particular
set of rules which constitute association football become the
most popular sport, and achieve such cultural pre-eminence?
What is the appeal of football as such?

The distinction between these two levels can also be stated
in terms of the hopes of the football crowd. One may watch in
the hope that a particular side will win, or one may watch in the
hope of seeing skilful or exciting play. Typically, both modes of
watching exist within the individual spectator – we want our
side to win, and we want a good match. The relative importance
of the two kinds of hope will vary between different spectators,
but we can ask – and it is important to do so – which is the
dominant mode across the sport as a whole. Today, of course,
the 'crowd' of spectators extends far beyond the gates of the
ground. As televised football has become more important for
the popularity and finances of the sport than attendance at
matches, the balance between the two modes of watching has
probably shifted. The TV spectator is less likely to be strongly
partisan, and may take sides according to the quality of football
played rather than having a fixed allegiance to club or country.

Psychoanalysis, as the theory of the unconscious, has a lot
to say about the formation and nature of partisan attachments, and thus has an important part to play in understanding that level of the passion for football. The concepts of
identification, splitting and narcissism, among others, can all
illuminate the emotional life of the crowd and of the fan.
When Freud wrote 'Group Psychology and the Analysis of the
Ego' in 1921, he set out some ideas which continue in the
present day to be the basis of the psychoanalytic understanding of collective phenomena. We form groups, he said, when
we hand over to a leader our capacities for regulating our
own actions – our superego functions, as he was later to call
them, those capacities for self-control, restraint and moral
judgment. We do so because it is easier than tolerating
internal conflicts between our asocial or antisocial impulses
on the one hand, and our needs for social relationships on the
other. Thus freed of internal conflict and of responsibility for
ourselves, we are ready to do the leader's bidding, and to
behave in groups in ways that we would not as individuals.

In the technical language of psychoanalysis (in which

today one might use the term 'projective identification' in
this context), we 'project' the superego parts of ourselves
into the leader, with whom we then identify, and who – for
reasons of his or her own – is ready to 'accept' these
projections, that is, to assume the role of superego for all.
The process called 'splitting' is also involved here: we need
to idealise the leader and the group to which we belong,
and to direct all our bad feelings outwards, to people
outside of the group. So in the need to split good from
bad, we distinguish in-group from out-of-group.

Freud's view of groups and social movements was thus a
negative one, influenced no doubt by the fact that he was a
Jew witnessing and suffering the rise of fascism. His ideas
have led to some powerful analyses by others of fascism
and of present-day forms of hateful, racist passion. There
does not have to be an individual leader as such: an
ideology, a faith, or the image of a nation can play a similar
role – hence the destructiveness which can be unleashed
under the banner of a creed or nation. This approach
certainly has something to say about the emotional life of
the football crowd, most clearly about the ugly forms of
that life at its violent and chauvinistic margins. It may be
that the development of theories of mass psychology by
Freud and others was influenced not only by the spectre of
the crowd in political turmoil, and especially by the fascist
mob, but also by the early experience of the crowd in
unruly pursuit of leisure. Massive football crowds were
becoming a regular part of everyday life in many countries
at the time Freud wrote his essay on group dynamics,
having occurred first in Britain in the 1890s.

However, nasty though football crowds can be, and blind
though many fans' idealisations of their own clubs may be,
there is much about the football crowd that escapes this kind
of analysis, with its stress on the psychological defects of
group membership. As well as these defects, there is a benign
quality to the development in the individual of the partisan
passions of football. For many of the boys who come to love
football, it is an expression of a local patriotism based simply
on a love of one's own place, and not involving a hatred of
other people's places and teams. We have no reason to
assume that this has completely died since poignant photographs of short-trousered boys with rosettes, rattles and
innocent smiles were taken in the 1950s and 1960s; similar

boys are to be seen in the stands today. And while the crowds which mill around grounds now contrast visually with the sombre uniformity of the cloth-capped masses at inter-war matches, the same spontaneous orderliness is there (and the same occasions of its breakdown), and the same rapture.

Moreover the contribution of psychoanalysis to understanding the partisan level of football feeling will tell us little about football itself. It will tell us how reserves of primitive group feeling become attached to the game, but not *why* they do: not where the rapture comes from. This chapter will focus primarily on this second level, that of football's intrinsic appeal, aside from and prior to its role as the vehicle for partisan identifications, though we will be returning to aspects of football as a social problem.

THE FOUNDING TABOO

To explore the bases of the passion for the actual game of football, we must look at the origins of the game. We need to examine the social and psychological meanings of the core elements of the code which for one hundred and thirty years has in a relatively stable way defined what football is. The laws of the game were first codified in Britain, as the code of the Football Association. In October 1863, the last of a series of reportedly stormy meetings took place at the Freemasons' Tavern in Great Queen Street, London, attended mainly by a number of ex-public schoolboys. The consequences of this meeting for the subsequent history of the world are considerable. It was decided at the meeting to form the Football Association, which was not only an organisational initiative but also, and crucially, was a decision about the nature of the game.[2]

There were several different varieties of football at the time, each major public school having evolved its own form of the game. Team games governed by consistent rules were introduced into the public schools to enhance the mental and physical development of the future members of the British ruling class (Mason, 1981), and to facilitate pupils' acceptance of the masters' authority (Dunning, 1971). Thus, as Dunning and others have described, organised football, as a replacement for the brutal, anarchic ball games previously played at the public schools, was part of what the sociologist

Norbert Elias (1939) has called the 'civilising process' – the growth of more restrained, civil and non-destructive forms of behaviour (Elias and Dunning, 1971).

In the late 1840s, a number of different forms of football had been gathered together into a single code by undergraduates at Cambridge, who wanted to be able to play together even though they had come from different public schools. The gradual move towards standardisation continued, pushed as ever by the need for a common set of rules if teams were ever to be able to play against others who did not share the same institutional origins. Furthermore, as well as the public school and university teams, there were soon many teams formed representing local communities. These had often been set up by churchmen or industrialists who wanted to bring some order and some physically beneficial activity into the emerging leisure time of the working classes (the Saturday half-holiday spread during the second half of the nineteenth century and was an essential precondition for the rise of football – see Mason, 1981).

A major step in the standardisation of football was taken at the 1863 meeting, when in the face of stiff opposition from some quarters it was decided to institute two prohibitions: one on handling the ball, and the other on what was called 'hacking' – kicking at the opponent rather than the ball. The idea of a total ban on handling had been introduced at Eton in 1849, probably (suggests Dunning) as an attempt to gain for Eton the leadership in this field which its staff and pupils assumed it should have in all fields. A little earlier Rugby School had seized the initiative by codifying its own form of the game, in which hacking was allowed, as was not merely handling but – unusually – actually running while holding the ball. So although the Rugby code imposed considerable restraints compared with how the game had usually been played hitherto, the Eton rules constituted a much further, dramatic move in the direction of greater self-restraint.

In the 1863 meeting there was most debate about hacking, the defenders of which – some of whom also wanted to preserve the right to handle – subsequently went their own way and formed the Rugby Football Union. However, as the psychologist R.W. Pickford (1940) suggested, since this group also came to outlaw hacking not long after, it is reasonable to suppose that the key issue was that of handling. It is this which came to be the most fundamental separation between the rugby and association codes.

In 1877 agreement was reached between the London F.A. and the other major organisation playing a similar game based in Sheffield, where football had been organised since the 1850s. Some Sheffield rules (including the corner kick) were incorporated into the F.A. code, thus laying the North–South foundation for a properly national organisation, and helping to secure adherence to the F.A. code by the burgeoning working-class participants in the game.

Further changes followed. Some were in the direction of further restraint; for example, until 1893 the goalkeeper could still be charged when not in possession of the ball. Others embodied further rationalisation, for instance the decision in 1889 that referees – who were becoming increasingly important – could give free kicks without there having been an appeal from the side against whom the foul had been committed. Thus the abstract body of law came increasingly to regulate play on the field.

But it seems that the core elements of football had already been emerging in the 1860s and 1870s, and the most central of these was the prohibition on handling, the taboo on touching as Pickford and others have suggested we might view it. It was intensified in 1912 when goalkeepers were banned from using their hands outside of the penalty area. If the ban on handling were definitive in football's emergence as a specific practice, we should be able to throw light on the intrinsic appeal of football if we inquire into the psychological significance of this taboo.

We can assume that the taboo is over-determined; this is a basic principle of psychoanalytic work, according to which the meaning of a psychological phenomenon such as a symptom or a dream cannot be reduced to a single cause. So the taboo on touching may stand for a number of different things. We will look here at only two of them.

Firstly, few human activities do not depend on the hands, and prohibiting their use forces the players into using their feet in new ways in order to move the ball around. In insisting on the creative use of the foot, football transforms what little conventional utility that part of the body has, apart that is from its obvious basic function in enabling us to stand and walk. When not simply facilitating human bipedalism, the foot is most often an instrument of violence. Phrases like 'putting the boot in' and 'a kick in the teeth', and our imagery of violent assaults in which the victim is kicked on the ground, testify to the conventional meaning of the foot as associated with primitive aggression. To play football, in which kicking an opponent is strictly prohibited and in which the ball can be moved around only by using the feet, one has to sublimate the murderous meaning of the foot, and to find other uses for this destructive appendage. Football is a 'civilising' influence in a psychological sense, then, as well as in the social-historical sense referred to above.

As Daniel Dervin (1985) points out, this can of course be said of all sporting activities which involve self-punishing regimes of training and self-mastery. The aggression is directed primarily at the self, in programmes of heroic self-improvement and preparation. And even in the perform-ance, it is not released directly at the opponent: what is sought is not the aggressive triumph of annihilating or gaining revenge over the opponent, but the narcissistic triumph of glory in victory (and failing that, in defeat). Dervin also suggests, contrary to conservative views of television as encouraging exhibitionism and promoting dis-plays of violence, that the increased televising of sport has led to increased restraint, since people on the whole do not want to be seen by millions engaging in unjustified aggres-sion. The use of video recordings to assist adjudication in cases of misbehaviour on the pitch will presumably, like the police cameras now increasingly placed along roads, add weight to any restraining influences at work.

Admittedly in football as in other sports more than a trace of the primitive aggression may still be experienced as such, not in the competitive urge to win, which itself is – or should be – a highly worked-over and 'civilised' form of aggression. The violence lingers rather in the relationship to the ball, which is repeatedly struck with considerable force and some-times to great dramatic effect. Yet the ball must not be – and is not – damaged, and moreover the overall experience of kicking or watching a football being kicked yields a language of expressive artistry more often than one of brutal attack: the deft, curling pass, the delicate chip and the accurately weighted, floating long ball make up far more of the game than explosive, cannon-like shots at goal. Skilful players 'hug' and 'stroke' the ball, and deliver it 'sweetly' to each other.

Freud suggested that sexual energy or libido ('Eros') can be deployed in different ways and concentrations in different parts of the body, to form the so-called 'erotogenic' zones. If we allow ourselves a little loose analogising, we might see the distribution of the aggressive energies, or 'Thanatos' as some writers have called our destructive impulses, as forming 'thanatogenic' zones. In football, the thanatogenic zone of the foot therefore undergoes an erotic transformation into an instrument of creativity. This modification of aggressive energies is perhaps aided by our memories of how as babies we express vigour and obtain pleasure through kicking movements, as well as using our feet to struggle against a restraining parent.

There is too a sexual dimension to football. The ultimate aim of all the kicking is, of coure, penetration of the other – specifically, penetration of a sacred or forbidden zone through an orifice. 'Scoring', as in slang parlance, is at one level a (male) sexual conquest. This is not unique to football – several games are organised around the objective of placing an object in a space or hole defended against such intrusion by the opponents or by natural barriers. The use of posts and netting to define that space, and so incidentally to enhance its orifice-like qualities, is also found in other games. Hockey, which crystallised a decade or so later than football, has similar strategic objectives, and a key prohibitory axiom (the ball can be moved only by striking with the hockey stick). It has, though, a more assaultive quality, in the use of a large stick to thrash a small, hard ball, and to tangle with an opponent's stick.

In football there is a lot more to kicking a ball around than the ultimate achievement of a sexual union through scoring a goal; there is an extension of human powers. Again, this is common to other ball games as well, insofar as they involve the tendency to try to make the ball a part of the self. Basketball, for example, involves direct, but highly constrained, contact with the ball, requiring finely developed ball-control skills. One of the most exciting spectacles in football, of which Maradona and Gascoigne on a good day are amongst the best recent exponents, is close control of the ball when moving at speed, such that the ball behaves as if it were a part of the player's body, as if the player has incorporated something external into himself. 'Dribbling' is an odd term, but it does suggest a close bodily link between player and ball. We are excited by the apparently magical incorporative achievements of dribbling and ball control, all the more so because we know them to be achievements of skill not magic. Simply picking up the ball and running with it, as in rugby, is prosaic in contrast. Though it has its own exhilarations, it does not provide the sense of transcendent mastery – and the vulnerability of that mastery to dissolution – which football does.

> Usually the ball has responded reasonably to my desires. At times it has seemed to anticipate my every wish and flowed so smoothly that I thought it a part of me and that the whole world lay obedient at my feet. But there have been times when it would bounce awkwardly and I had despairing days fighting the unseen forces that bedevilled it. (Danny Blanchflower, 1958)

In association football is there a complete ban on ten of eleven players touching the ball by hand while on the field of play. All sports must in some way be based on prohibitions, but this is a very extreme prohibition, and since it determines the nature of the game then the popularity of football must be related to the psychological meaning of this particular taboo. It has been suggested so far that one of its meanings is the sublimation of aggression, achieved in such a way that includes some sexual and magical excitements. There is now a second, though related, meaning to discuss, which takes us to the heart of football, and not only of football.

RE-ENACTING COMMUNITY

Taboos have played an important part in psychoanalytic thinking: Freud himself was very interested in them, both as symptoms – as in the avoidance of certain everyday objects in obsessional neurosis – and as cultural institutions, particularly as documented by the anthropological writers avidly read by Freud. He remarked that in both obsessional neuroses and in cultural taboos, the principal prohibition is against touching, and the anthropological evidence which he was reviewing certainly suggested that it was of paramount importance among taboo practices. The difference between the neurotic symptom and the cultural precept, he suggested in 'Totem and

Taboo' (1913, p. 73), is that in the neurosis the prohibition relates to sexual touching, while cultural taboos are more concerned with repressing the aggressive, controlling aims of touching, that is, with proscribing touch as the necessary precursor of attack or appropriation.

Later (in 'Inhibitions, Symptoms and Anxiety', 1926) he revised this view to accommodate also the neurotic's struggle against the aggression with which obsessionality is undoubtedly infused. The taboo object is both desired and hated, both in neurotic symptom and in cultural institution. Nonetheless, grounds for differentiating the neurotic from the cultural remain, in that Freud had earlier also seen the symptom as a private, asocial struggle with instinctual need: the neurotic turns away from the real world of human society into the phantasy expressed by the symptom – that disaster will result if contact is made with the desired but forbidden object. The cultural constructions of taboos, on the other hand, are themselves formative of human community, the fabric of which may indeed be seriously damaged if they are infringed. Societies are necessarily constituted around taboos of various kinds.

As is well known, in Freud's own thinking on this matter the taboo on incest is seen as of especial significance, as being elemental to the very existence of human society. The incest taboo obviates destructive competition between the brothers of the primal horde after their parricide, and unites them in a reparative reimposition upon themselves of their dead father's will. Also the exogamy which follows from it has been seen as the basis of exchange and sociality between family groups (Mitchell, 1974).

However, it is not necessary to accept Freud's historical anthropology in full in order to derive from his observations on taboos the notion that a taboo-like prohibition is a primal form of law, a rudiment of human society because of the way it helps us to manage our impulses. It is a drastic and blunt instrument, but such is the quality of the primitive psychic processes with which it has to deal. The taboo on killing others would scarcely be questioned as a prerequisite for human community, yet its inadequacy as an absolute rule generates many problems of decision which are the stuff of philosophical and legal discussions about when it may be right or excusable to kill.

In sport, we echo the formative moment of human

society by imposing upon ourselves taboos or rules which we must observe for at least the greater part of the time if it is to be at all possible to play the game. Of all the sports which were codified in the late nineteenth century and accrued some mass following, football acquired its pre-eminence, and became the 'people's game', because it was based on the most stringent taboo, the one requiring most restraint not only in its prohibition of direct aggression but also in the very elimination from play of the human hand. The exception is of course in the entirely special and completely defensive role of the goalkeeper – and once the goalkeeper holds the ball, play in a sense is suspended. The ball is then safe and neutralised, and for a brief period is no longer a dangerous or exciting object.

Of course a handball can, depending on the circumstances, be a relatively trivial infraction, when it does not threaten the whole basis of the game. In contrast the famous handling offence by Maradona which went unnoticed by the referee and led to England's defeat in the 1986 World Cup semi-final against Argentina has become emblematic of a deep corruption of football. We may suspect this was not only because of its direct consequence for England but also because it was tantamount to someone picking up the ball and throwing it in the goal. This is the most obvious and effective way to put the ball in the net, and is a direct subversion of the founding principle of the game, which consists precisely in the necessity of taking a more indirect route to score. Maradona's post-match comment also helped to draw out the symbolic meaning of his action: it was 'the hand of God', he said – perhaps a joke, or an unwitting remark, about his own egotism, but also an implicit recognition that no human, social authority could sanction his action, or knowingly overlook it. The very possibility of any human, social endeavour rests on axioms of conduct being consistently upheld, and transgressions brought to book. As the imperial English would have said of Maradona's action, 'it wasn't cricket', though their sense of what constituted both cricket and society was a very partisan one. Certainly what Maradona did was not football.

It does not matter, at one level, what the content of the taboo is in any particular sport: the existence of any elemental rule of play will be sufficient to simulate human community. Thus football's taboo is to some degree a formal and empty one, in that although the taboo on handling is rich in

potential meanings, the actual object of the taboo in this case
– the ball – does not lend itself particularly clearly to
association with any specific unconscious meaning.

It is however available for a variety of associations, which
have been explored by a number of writers, notably by the
psychoanalyst Adrian Stokes (1956) in a rich paper on the
meanings of ball-games. It is the phallus or semen which
enters the forbidden orifice; it is the severed head, a
sado-masochistic image of castration and domination; it is,
in the course of being repeatedly put into motion, an
expression of life – and if so, ball-games provide for men
the opportunity symbolically to emulate women by giving
life to something. This is a very speculative observation by
Daniel Dervin (1985), but we have nothing firmer to go on
in the search for the intrapsychic meanings of men's greater
participation in ball games. Another interesting speculation
of Dervin's is that the ball represents helplessness; we can
project into it and split off our feelings of our own
helplessness, and are then freed to develop our skills and
mastery by gaining control over it.

On the other hand, Marcelo Suarez-Orozco (1993) stresses
the phallic functions of the ball. A 'recovered' football fan, he
analyses some typical chants of Argentinian football crowds
and concludes that the appeal of football is that it dramatizes
scenes of homosexual intercourse – the orifice, defended at
the rear, is not the vagina but the male anus. (In one
particularly clear example, a chant depicts the victory of a
team as the prick of its manager up the arse of the opposing
team's manager.) The football match enables spectators to
experience vicariously the triumphs – and the fears – associated with homosexuality in a culture where the active, pen-
etrative homosexual role is seen as consistent with machismo,
while the passive one is an ultimate form of humiliation.

From a British standpoint it might be suggested that as
an explanation of football's major appeal this is not compelling. While shame at having let the opponent get in at the
back may be a common feeling, there is no evidence that
this is primarily associated with homosexuality. The experience of scoring or letting in goals is not, in the British
discourse of football, linked with a 'breaking ass' kind of
triumphalism, whatever resonance that may have, as Suarez-
Orozco's account suggests, in South America.

All of these associations to the meaning of the ball are

consistent with the fertile suggestion made by Helene Deutsch in 1926, that sport converts neurotic anxieties into real ('out-there') anxieties, and so provides an opportunity to manage them. The original anxiety is lodged in the matter to be mastered, or in the opponent, and can then in principle be controlled. (Deutsch offered this general idea in writing of a patient with severe castration anxiety and associated fear of death, overcome partly by his development of an intense involvement with ball games, in which the ball symbolised the castrating hand of the father.) Even when one loses, by identification with the victor and with the game as a whole one can be reassured of the possibility of mastering the anxieties (though perhaps the recurrent difficulty in doing this explains why the defeat of one's team can have the aura of personal disaster for the fan).

Though in different contexts we may find evidence for any and all of these psychic meanings of the ball, overall perhaps the main thing about a spherical ball (unlike the oval one of the rugby code) is its predictable neutrality. It will bounce without favour, and similarly it does not favour any particular symbolic meaning. Early footballs were often made of animal organs, especially pig's bladders, but we should probably not make too much of this.

Yet there is ambivalence towards the ball, as there is towards real taboo objects, whether obsessional or phobic. It is both to be possessed as much as possible, by the team if not by every individual player, and yet is perpetually knocked away from oneself. You want to get it, and you want to get rid of it. We have noted the necessary violence meted out to the ball, but also the loving, artistic uses of it, the experience of kicking as caressing rather than smiting. We have also commented on the effort to make the ball a part of oneself. Perhaps we should consider the ball not only as a taboo object but also as what the psychoanalyst Donald Winnicott (1951) called a 'transitional object', something which is experienced both as a part of the self and as part of the external world. The ball is a part of the external world, but in itself a bland and insignificant part. Only through creative work upon it in a culturally given context does it become important and meaningful, as an object which is experienced both as a part of oneself and as otherness, as an element of shared culture.

At root, however, whatever the ball at particular moments

might stand for as a desired or hated object, the main thing about football's taboo is not so much its content but its extent. Football involves a very severe prohibition, and a high degree of restraint, and so it is a highly suitable medium through which we can experience over and over again what it is to be a member of a society, any society, indeed what it is to be human. As one famous saying has it, football isn't a matter of life and death; it's more important than that. Or we can consider another proposition by Danny Blanchflower (who played for Aston Villa, Spurs and Northern Ireland in the 1950s and early 1960s), that football is not about winning, but about glory (Hill, 1989, pp. 6–7).

A further famous aphorism about the essence of the game puts a different view, that in football winning is not the main thing, it's the only thing. At stake here is the deep conflict which has run through the history of the game, and of most other sports, which was historically defined as that between 'professional' and 'amateur' outlooks, the former being interested primarily in winning, since livelihoods may depend on success on the field. It corresponds in part to the distinction made earlier between the partisan and the intrinsic satisfactions of the game. The 'amateur' view expressed by Blanchflower is arguably the more profound one. The glory in question is not the partisan glory of scoring the winning goal, but the glory of the whole spectacle as an instance of human society. This can be echoed in the winners' pride and the partisan celebrations can be a kind of civic festival, as when the victorious Cup winning team returns to its home. But more generally, and apart from the pleasures and pains of winning and losing, spectators can participate as much as the players in the affirmation of society which organised sport represents, even while stirring cups of tea in their own living rooms.

To put this psychoanalytically, there is an identification with an image of society, an image carried and realised by the sport, with its rituals, its agonistic encounters and above all its taboos and rules. Sport is then a kind of secular equivalent of religion, if we adopt Durkheim's view of religion as our worship of society, or rather of society and its powers as projected into the image of the deity. The glory of football resides in its particular capacity to evoke in us an awe of civilisation. It deploys libidinal and aggressive forces before us, but in a contained way; it provides also the abstract authority – the lines on the field, the rules and the referee – before which those forces must yield, but within whose provenance they can be expressed.

To some extent, this is an idealisation of society, as a place where some win and some lose but basically everything is wonderful. However there are different degrees and kinds of idealisation. It can be more or less brittle and defensive. It is probably more so in the case of those who want to 'keep politics out of sport', who cannot tolerate the linking of the idealised world of sport with the real world of human society and its painful conflicts and shortcomings. As in psychic life generally, the least pathological situation is that in which the idealising impulse is subordinated as much as possible to the reality principle – that is to say, we must start from what the world is really like, and obtain our narcissistic satisfactions not from constructing ideal images of our present or future selves but from grappling with the real world. Football culture in itself can help this tendency along by giving due recognition to the real social conflicts that inevitably enter into it, rather than treating them as distasteful irrelevancies, as for example most football commentators have tended to treat racism.

So the passion for football stems at least in part from the game's representing to us the extraordinary and powerful fact of human community. Furthermore, as described earlier, another key feature of the early codification of football, aside from the no-handling rule, was the progressive elimination of violence towards other players, thus taking it a very long way from the often recklessly combative games of street football that had existed in villages for centuries, and from the bloody wall and field games of public schools. In this way also, then, football represents the claim upon us of human society and its more exacting, sophisticated restraints.

At the same time, it is still a game of great physical robustness. Strength in shoulder to shoulder combat and in shielding the ball, power in the air, tenacity in tackling and in riding tackles, speed, and stamina, all contribute to playing excellence. It also has a rich vocabulary of muscular sensuality – of swerving, leaping and other athletic performances, and of a discourse of skill very similar to dancing – the pirouette, the jigging or swaying run, and so on. In many photographs of footballers there is a strongly balletic quality to the moment captured; the boy fan may not know

of Degas' ballerinas, but he has his cigarette-card centre-
forwards (or, now, his *SHOOT!* magazine strikers) who have
just as much grace.

Football is an example of how the most compelling cultural
practices and artefacts that we have are those which one way
or another combine high degrees of both the socially constrained and the bodily primitive – discipline and the erotic,
cooperation and the aggressive. Furthermore, as it has developed and become more technical and more sophisticated,
both its social and bodily dimensions have been enhanced.
Professional football now involves very high levels of technical
and emotional teamwork along with, in the diverse imagery of
potency, fecundity and endurance that it supports, a great
richness of bodily expression.

RE-ENACTING LOSS

Sport in general, and football in particular, is then at once a
re-enactment and libidinisation of community, and a civilisation of libido. There is another way of stating this, closer to
the core concerns of contemporary psychoanalysis, which
brings a different aspect to light. This is that participation in
or enthusiastic watching of a sporting game involves some
repeated experience of disappointment and some confrontation with loss.

This is obviously true at the partisan level: in the game as
a whole, there is as much losing as winning, and even winning
sides must often endure giving away some goals on the road
to victory. Nick Hornby's (1992) autobiographical account of
his relationship to football brings into focus an element of the
popular feeling for football which is well known to any fan
but has not hitherto been brought into writing and intellectualising about the game. He writes of being struck during his
first visits to matches by the frequent complaining and
bitterness about him on the terraces, and observes that
'Entertainment as pain was an idea entirely new to me, and it
seemed to be something I'd been waiting for' (p. 21). Many
of the people around him shouted and cursed as if they *hated*
being there. In the subsequent development of his passion,
Hornby came to realise that he did not go to matches for fun:
boring football (of which his team, Arsenal, have been
generous providers) was as compelling as any virtuoso per-

formance (p. 135). Protesting about it he likens to protesting that *King Lear* has a sad ending. So the sense of resignation with which the true enthusiast approaches football applies also to its aesthetic as well as partisan dimensions; beauty and poetry may be as elusive as victory. Hornby's understanding of this is that football provides not an escape or relief from the world but an 'alternative universe', as serious, varied and disillusioning as the worlds of work or personal relationships. People at football are therefore as 'panicky and glum' (p. 136) as in other contexts.

In a very different register, Stokes (1956) makes some related points. In cricket (which was obviously his favourite sport), the regular experience of losing your wicket entails 'the repeated endurance of symbolic castration', while many sports bring 'unexpected tribulation' (p. 185), and mimic the 'degree of fitfulness from which in adult life we had best learn to contrive nourishment' (p. 188). He suggests that in games we can allow ourselves to experience loss and disappointment in ways which do not bring the full weight of these psychic traumas upon us. To draw a parallel with ideas which another psychoanalyst, Donald Winnicott, was advancing in the 1950s, we might say that sporting contests present us with the world in small doses, as the mother does for the baby, with painful exposure to unwelcome reality in proportions which we can manage without recourse to defensive illusions. Arguably as adults we also need the larger doses from time to time, the full confrontations with destructiveness or despair which drama and literature (whether in 'high' or popular culture) might provide us with. But this does not require us to belittle the psychic role played by the moderate quotidian dosage of reality staged for us by such spectacles as football.

Like the mother, sport must also offer some compensations, something in return for our tolerance of reality and the losses and limits it imposes upon us. Hornby identifies a number of the gains he made in his peer relationships from his immersion in football, although he is alert to its 'retardant' effect, its role in his frightened hanging-on to his schoolboy self. Also, one interesting feature of his account is the way in which he links his feelings for Arsenal with his family history, his passion for a football team arriving both to fill a gap left by his father after his parents separated, and to maintain a link with his father who took him to matches.

Yet the emotional compensations must be deeper and more

universal than this, important though such specific functions
may be for many individuals. Both Stokes and Dervin hint at
the capacity of sporting participation (as player or spectator)
to relive a fundamental developmental process, and thus to
confirm us in our achievements in having – to some extent at
least – grown up. Dervin writes that the boundaries involved
in any sport, and concretely present in white lines on turf,
'suggest the very earliest operations of the self emerging from
the maternal environment'. Their inviolability recalls the most
archaic level of ego formation, the first apprehensions by the
emergent self of the intractable otherness of reality. Behaving
with respect for the boundaries of the game can thus provide
us with the same satisfactions as the young ego: the pleasures
of autonomy, of knowing what one is and relating to an other
and others in an ordered way, of knowing what to do, and
above all of belonging, of having a place within a containing
social matrix.

For Stokes, the white lines of the playing field have an
architectural significance: they connote a home space, a
building, and ultimately the mother's body, upon which the
players play and to which they give a new life. And as with
the mother's body, sensual properties belonging to our experience of the physical nature of the field (the luxuriance and
exhilaration of grass) are inextricably linked with the demands
of social being – the otherness of it, and the lawful nature of
what one may do on or with it. If we can accept both of
these facets, it can give us pleasure, support and space. This
space is very clearly and firmly bounded: the game must be
suspended if non-players invade the pitch; the 'touch-line' in
football marks a taboo zone which has to be observed from
both sides.

Our readiness to accept and benefit from 'these nourishing
architectural limitations', Stokes implies, are enhanced by the
multiple identifications which the players (and spectators)
make with each other, since both teams include all roles, and
all players know the experiences which others are going
through. The emergent sum of interwoven and reciprocal
identifications is a collective identification with the game
itself, a sort of corporate psyche which binds participants not
only to their team but to the code and community of the
sport. Stokes does not conceptualise this along the Freudian
lines of a regressively disowned superego, but strikes a more
positive note in references to a 'profound unity' and to an

image of the game as providing 'an all-embracing element linked with life at the breast'. There is regression here, of course, but in the service of a rule-bound encounter with reality, its countless petty restrictions, its occasional dramatic gifts and penalties, and its opportunities to relate to others. As sport cultivates aggression in the service of narcissism, so also does it deploy regressive narcissism in the service of fundamental sociability.

This enables us to locate the obvious homoerotic elements of football (the affections showered upon goal-scorers, and other rituals[3]) in a wider framework, as more feelings of early narcissistic origin which are incorporated into a fundamentally social and reality-based experience.

The relinquishing of omnipotence, the giving up of early illusions, is the psychic basis of social membership. In re-enacting loss, and containing our responses to it, we are therefore rehearsing the basis of community. The lost mother of the world of omnipotent, infantile experience is mourned in countless cultural forms, and memories of her transmuted into resources for realistic and creative living. Popular cultural practices partake of this process as widely and deeply as any form of art.

PARTISANSHIP

Let us return now to the starting-point, and reconsider the other level at which football must also be understood – that of partisanship. As we do so the psychoanalytic dimension will be partly absorbed into a set of historical, cultural and political concerns. This is intentional and desirable. Psycho-analytic insights into societal phenomena stand their best chance of being heard if they build themselves around the knowledge of social processes gained in other disciplines, and if they can take their place in non-esoteric forms of public debate.

Many issues at this other level need clarifying, since the patterns of partisan attachments which have been organised around football are complex, and have changed with time. While it may be possible to link football historically to the phenomenon of working-class consciousness, and especially to working-class images of masculinity, this is at best only a part of the story. The 50 per cent decline in attendances at

Football League matches in the post-war period is certainly related to the gradual decomposition of the industrial working-class, yet by other indices – not least the size of audiences for televised football – the game is as popular as ever. Furthermore, the middle and upper classes created the game, and were prominent in its early history, while lower middle class support has always been an important feature of football culture. And at the level of ownership, football clubs have never been working-class institutions.

As for gender, there have always been girl and women fans, and they are increasing in numbers and articulacy (there is at least one magazine for female fans in Britain). At least 10,000 women regularly play organised football (Mason, 1989) – another recent estimate (*The Observer*, 9 December 1990) is 45,000; the top games are now televised, and a national league is planned. In Scandinavia women already play football to a much greater extent, while in Italy there is a professional women's league.

The passion for place is also complex. While most League clubs were founded as local institutions, and continue to generate intense local feeling, for some time some of the most passionate supporters of the larger clubs have had little or no connection with the place represented by the club. Further, some of the ugliest identifications made by football fans are not with the team nor the town at all, but with the particular territorial and sub-cultural sections of the crowd to which they belong – the 'Shed', the 'Firm', the 'End' and so forth.

So although we can expect a psychoanalytic approach to throw light on all varieties of partisan passion, such an approach has to take account of the contextual complexities. Partisanship in football is not a simple matter. This will be especially so if the ideas advanced here about the intrinsic appeal of football are correct. For they suggest that there is a deep connection between the two levels of football's appeal. On the one hand football is the vehicle of some of today's most powerful partisan identities. On the other, it has an intrinsic appeal, a major part of which is that it mimics society as a whole; it embodies a high level of development of the civilising process, and is a dramatic representation of the psychic capacities which are at the root of all our attachments to particular identities. There must then be an important interaction between the two levels, between the formation of specific attachments and the affirmation of the general capacity for attachment of any kind. As we have seen, the identification with the team, and the identification with society as represented by the whole match and its context, both rest to some extent on idealisation.

Yet at the same time it is important to maintain the distinction between the two. Idealisations can differ importantly in quality, being more or less defensive, and their social import will differ also according to their object – compare the fascist politics of an emotional investment in an idealised 'white Great Britain', purged of bad elements, with the democratic politics, albeit not unproblematically so, of an attachment to an image of an idealised 'multiracial Britain', purged of conflict. The extent to which football – like any other sport – is a constructive and reconciliatory force in society depends upon its universal, intrinsic appeal outweighing its appropriation by partisan sentiments (necessary and at times constructive though the latter may be). The glory of the game, the idealisation of society, must outweigh the glory of winning, the idealisation of the group.

The most destructive modern form of partisan feeling is racism, and as we know football has provided many occasions for racist passions to exert themselves. Moreover the British Asian communities, among the most vulnerable to racism, are not (at least not yet) a major part of the professional football world here, mainly because football is not a street game in the countries from which British Asians originally came. It is, however, in the Caribbean countries, and the now routine presence of black players in most League sides and in the British national teams has gone some way to undercut terrace racism, at least towards Afro-Caribbeans. Although 'monkey chanting' (the practice of making rapid hooting noises when a black player gets possession of the ball) may still be heard it is a less powerful force than the positive excitement of watching black players in action.

Moreover this kind of excitement, though it springs from the inherent aesthetics of football, is enhanced for many of us by its specific social meaning, by the fact that here we have black men claiming a place in a game which was at the heart of traditional white British culture. On a wider canvas and over time, many other ethnicities and nationalities have appropriated and added to the traditions of skill and effort which the game embodies. As a consequence football has been made available as a universal aesthetic of the modern world, a global medium for the affirmation of a common humanity under a shared taboo.

The force of the taboo rests not only on the negative threat of exclusion or punishment. It also derives from the positive experience of observing it, from the delights of participation. The 'ref' on any particular day may be a hated or contemptible figure, but the laws and traditions of the game are a bountiful authority, creating and maintaining a space for bodily expression and pleasurable encounter. These laws and traditions have their faults and are not immutable, but insofar as they are experienced as basically good and providing, then they are an external, institutionalised form of a good parental object.

This has not meant that the love for football is necessarily a pro-establishment force; the good society which it is felt to represent is not typically experienced as the actual existing social order. On the contrary, as we have been noting, it may still often be experienced as a class- or place-limited collectivity, however little material basis there may now be for such experience. The presence at club board level of high-profile representatives of the capitalist class may be profoundly resented by some supporters. Yet even when the goodness and community which the game represents is defined in an explicitly oppositional way (as 'our' game, embodying better values than 'they' represent) its psychic meanings of reconciliation with others must exert a universalising pull on the emotions.

The role that football plays in symbolising so powerfully the general fact of society and of social authority may explain why it has been a focus of social disorder. It is debatable, as Geoffrey Pearson (1983) has shown, whether the disorder around football has in fact increased significantly over the whole period of its development.[4] Still, whatever the quantitative trend, there are grounds for taking the existence of self-consciously violent sub-cultures specifically organised around football as a relatively recent development. To talk of violent 'football fans' is seriously inaccurate here, since the pursuit of the violence is often at the expense of experiencing the game itself. Offenders may be arrested before or during a game, or the match itself may be interrupted. It would be more reasonable to infer that the serious 'hooligan' hates football, and is doing what he can to destroy it. This is in a sense a displacement, in that the underlying or original hatred is of society. Usually, however, in displacement, there is little or no awareness of the original feeling, whereas here the hatred of society is likely to be more acknowledged than that of football. Participants in this hatred seem to be brutalised (though not necessarily impoverished) young working-class men who hate society partly for the cultural dispossession or deracination which recent socio-economic changes have wrought upon them. Their attacks upon football (either directly, upon the pitch and players, or indirectly, through the spoiling effects of their disturbances) are an impotent attack upon the social order as a whole symbolised by football.

The extreme, panicky reactions to football-associated violence may also be better understood in this light. Attention has been given in recent years to football as the site of radical breakdowns of community, in the triumphs of the 'hooligans' over the restraining authorities. The seriousness of some of these breakdowns should not be underestimated, and some of the accounts of disorder produced by social researchers in the 1970s seem now like sentimental illusions, in their implications that terrace life was a form of spirited working-class resistance that did not involve real violence. But the mainstream ordered world of football, at all its levels, continued through these marginal, though distressing, intrusions. Nonetheless, it was seen by many as being in a state of widespread, terminal violence, which threatened to infect the wider society.

This fearful perception, while fed in part by a class-based distaste for the game, may, like the attacks to which it is a response, also have stemmed from the fact of football's symbolic importance. When such a powerfully good object, which has been so important in the constitution of the contemporary social order is abused, by however few people, strong anxieties are aroused. Was the object that good after all, or has football ever been mainly an excuse for loutishness? Or if it was that good, but it cannot contain the 'hooligans', then what hope is there for the survival of any social authority? Underlying both these questions is the anxiety that sensuality and competitiveness, sexuality and aggression, cannot be contained – that neither sublimation nor reparation can be sustained. Sport in some form will presumably continue to provide a major reassurance that such containment is possible. The growing popularity of football in countries where it was more recently established, and of the

World Cup as a component of global culture, suggest that on a world-historical stage it has some time to go as a leading form of this reassurance.

Having made by now some general case for this appreciative socio-psychoanalytic account of football, I will append a personal recollection. This is of standing as a boy in a bus garage on damp, cold Saturday afternoons waiting for the 'football specials' which ferried people from the city centre to the football ground. There were long queues, groups of chattering and shouting boys dotted among the often silent men in their belted raincoats, usually a dirty beige or weak green in colour, the standard attire for the working man in those days. In the warm smell of diesel and cigarettes, I was happily experiencing a quietly pleasurable solidarity. This was in part a class-based and gendered identification, but was also a more universal sense of community, of occupying a place in an ordered social framework, objectionable though that framework was in many respects. An hour later the sun might have broken through and I was in a position high on the terraces admiring the flowing geometry of the game on the bright green turf below. But the excitement I felt then was of a piece with the earlier sense of belonging in the bus garage. Each experience required the other, neither could have occurred without the other. The passion for association football is inseparable from the passion for association.

4   THE BODY OF THE NATION

THE FIRST HOME

From the green turf of the football pitch to the green grass of
the countryside, which is the topic of this chapter,[1] is in a
number of ways a short step. In Britain, both are places of
leisure (among other things). And both have played important
roles in the popular consciousness of Britain as a nation.
Traditionally, the physical presence of people in these two
green spaces has been strongly influenced by class – the
workers pressed together on the terraces, the middle classes
seeking space around themselves in the countryside. The
latter may therefore seem out of place in a book on popular
culture; despite its earlier appeal to a wholesome, self-
improving fraction of the traditional working class, and its
growing attractiveness now to a wider, partly de-classified
consumer population (in, for example, the use of the farm as
a site for leisure and educational activities), the countryside is
not an object of mass consumption.

Images of the countryside are, however, very much a part
of the everyday consumer society, most conspicuously in the
content of advertising but also as the setting for much
television drama, for example. Mythologies of rural life and
visions of the English (and British) countryside are essential
to many everyday understandings of the 'national heritage'.
What will be examined in this chapter are the unconscious
dimensions of nationalistic meanings of the countryside, particularly those which merge into what are now racist defini-
tions of the British nation, in that they equate Britishness
with whiteness.

The starting point is what might be described (using what
now, in post-Marxist times, seems to be a rather old-
fashioned term) as a *contradiction* in the experience of many
socially sensitive and broadly anti-racist people in Britain
today. The contradiction is this: the countryside is often

looked to, at least by white people, as a source of pleasure
and of recuperative reverie. However in their identification
with non-white people,[2] British white people may experience
a surprising and unwelcome alienation from their green and
pleasant land. For black people the countryside does not as a
rule function as such a resource.

The problem is two-fold. There is firstly the relatively
infrequent presence of non-white people in many of the
villages and small towns of rural Britain, not to mention on
the bridleways and coastal paths. This means that although
instances of outright racism are rare, there is an almost
ubiquitous element of unease in response to the unfamiliarity
of a non-white presence. This may only be in passing, at the
moment of first contact. It may be evident in nothing more
than the intensity of the first glance. Very often people will
struggle with their feelings, and will go on to behave in a
resolutely normal way towards the non-white presence. If the
face is that of a child, some very solicitous behaviour may
follow. It is very hard to identify anything in the behaviour of
others which one could convincingly complain about. And yet
as a white person one imagines that the non-white person is
left with a sense of being different, exotic and not quite
belonging. So part of the problem is out there, in the
responses, however subtle, of others.

But a distinctive part of it is of a more internal nature, in
the feelings and phantasies which we all, black and white,
have about the countryside. A member of the Black Environment Network, an organisation concerned with the relationship of black people to the countryside, has summed up the
problem in expressing a wish that she could stand at the top
of Snowdon and feel at home. The problem here is not one of
unease caused by difficulties some whites may have in
relating to blacks in rural settings, but is more to do with the
phantasies evoked by those settings in themselves, and with
the question of whether someone can feel at home there. The
sense of home originates, like so much else, in early bodily
experience, or rather in the particular emotional and social
qualities through which our infantile bodies are mediated to
us. The body is the most enduring and irreducible home one
has. So to feel at home somewhere you have to feel that it –
the house, or town, or country – is an extension or reflection
of your body.

This chapter will explore the nature and the socio-historical roots of some shared phantasies (in the psychoanalytic sense of the unconscious imagination) about the homeliness – or otherwise – of the British countryside. The core of its argument is firstly that the countryside is experienced as a body, and secondly that it is experienced as a white body and therefore as un-homely for non-white persons.

The first of these statements is uncontroversial, or at least should be to a psychoanalytically oriented audience. We are continually making what can be called somatomorphic projections onto all the things that surround us, in particular many of the material objects we are in frequent contact with. One of the most pre-eminent material objects of the present day, the motor car, is manifestly understood in bodily terms, as will be discussed in the next chapter. We do not need psychoanalysis to tell us the importance of metaphors of the body in organising much everyday experience. Psychoanalysis does however have a distinctive contribution to make in illuminating the developmental origins of these metaphors and in identifying the key role they play throughout life in our mental processes and in determining action. Above all it can illuminate how these metaphors are not isolated phenomena but are embedded in our emotional lives and social relationships, and how they can tie together the intrapsychic and the intimate with events and processes – often very large-scale ones – in the public sphere.

So let us try to look in a broadly psychoanalytic way at the phantasy of the countryside as a body, and specifically as a white body. As always, vocabulary provides a major indication of underlying phantasy. Among the words used in the description of topographical features are head, neck, shoulder, back, finger, foot, mouth and brow. People speak of parks as lungs of urban areas, and of rivers and roads as arteries. The metaphors have not always had positive associations. The historian Keith Thomas (1983), in his work on attitudes towards the natural world, describes how in earlier times, before the modern pastoral idyll came to dominate our views of the countryside, and it was widely experienced as threatening or wasted space, parts of it – especially upland parts – were referred to as warts, boils, excrescences and pudenda.

Overall though there do not appear to be many common uses of words relating to the sexual organs to describe topographical features. In this connection, however, we should note the landscape across which Postman Pat makes his daily journeys. Postman Pat (see, e.g., Cunliffe and Berridge, 1987) is a cartoon character, an unusually benign fellow who delivers mail to people who live dotted around a wonderfully benign rural environment. There is something striking about the hills in this landscape, which are compact mounds bearing every resemblance to the female breast. They lack nipples, but the shape is unequivocal. Exaggerated though the likeness may be in this case, it illustrates a pervasive quality of our experience, namely the sense that we move and rest upon a surface which is that of a body, and which at the most fundamental level is a female body.

Incidentally Postman Pat appears to be set in the 1950s, which is increasingly represented in a wide range of contexts as the last moment of purity and innocence. In the case of the British countryside, there are some historical reasons for this fantasy, even though it is a fantasy (cf. *unconscious* 'phantasy', above, 'fantasy' is used here in the sense of a consciously experienced illusion, in this case a publicly shared one). The 1950s are seen as the last moment before the rural railway system was drastically reduced, and before motorways began to be laced across the land. Also, of particular relevance to the present chapter, it was the last period when, in urban areas at least, one could expect that the local post office was run by a Mrs Goggins and not by a Mr or Mrs Patel. But that is to move ahead of the argument.

Many parts of the British countryside may be experienced as a human body laid out before one, with gentle undulations and creases, and neat shapes of woodland like areas of hair. As important as the surface features is the impression of inner fecundity and richness which many of our British landscapes convey. The combination of tranquillity and sensuality evoked by such landscapes must to any psychoanalytic way of thinking be premissed upon the baby's experience at the breast.

In the small amount of writing by psychoanalysts on this subject there are conceptualisations of our experience of the countryside which are consistent with that offered here. Bob Hinshelwood (1993) suggests that variations from medieval times to the present in prevalent conceptions of the British countryside – which is seen as always paired with the town or city – can be understood as the expression of variations in prevalent unconscious phantasies of the parents in intercourse. The 'combined parent figure' is an important element in the Kleinian picture of unconscious phantasy life, with its origins in the infant's anxious and envious imaginings of the parents as a sexual couple. Much sadism and destructiveness is typically projected into the combined parental imago, which then takes on terrifying qualities. The infant's responses to it may take a number of forms, in which attempts are made – in phantasy – to separate the parents, or control their coming together.

Hinshelwood links the masculine and feminine components respectively to the city/town and countryside, suggesting that present-day fears about the 'rape' of the latter express the collapse of attempts to avert or control the violent intercourse. In medieval times it had been possible to keep hearth and town safely separate, in the popular imagination, from the dangerous heath; subsequently, early modern visions of the latter saw it as amenable to control and pacification, as in landscape gardening. Now the danger is seen not in the wilderness but in the (male) attack of technology and commerce upon the innocence and purity of nature.

The countryside may not always be so exclusively identified as female. Somewhere along the road, and very early on, the domain of the male body becomes interwoven with that of the female in our phantasy topography, perhaps initially through the occurrence of the characteristics of hardness and resistance in the land and earth.[3] It is also questionable whether the specific, very primitive configuration of the combined parental imago has been the most central one in the cultural 'collectivisation of phantasies', as Hinshelwood describes the link between psyche and society, or whether more benign visions of creative intercourse have not historically also played an important role. Nonetheless Hinshelwood's striking hypothesis is broadly consistent with the attempt here to ground our experience of the rural in the matrix of bodily experience.

Harold Searles (1960), in his work on the experience of the non-human environment, stresses the quality of 'relatedness' characteristic of the mature person's attitudes to the natural world, and sees this as similar to our healthy relations with human others. At best, we feel ourselves to be deeply related to, yet know we are separate from, the non-human material world. As in relationships with people, we can be nourished by it, and wish to care for it, but we are not lost in a sense of complete fusion with it. We have separated from it, in sadness and gratitude, as we have from the mother's body.

Regressed though we may be at moments of especially strong pleasure in the countryside, our general appreciation of it is not regressive. Much of the countryside, in Britain at least, embodies human labour and society – that is, the pains of work and separation – as much as it reminds us of a primitive bounty. Moreover, the body phantasies which are at work here are necessarily involved in all experience, energising and enriching all spheres of activity. But because of its material forms, and our material dependence on it, it is likely that images of the countryside are particularly infused with a sense of the mother's body. You 'come from' a particular region or country, often symbolised by landscapes; and also you identify with the land, where your roots are or your heart lies – it is, by projection (the unconscious externalisation of aspects of the self), your body, as well as your mother's (and your father's).

LABOUR AND CONTAGION

Why, then, should the countryside be experienced as a *white* body? If it is seen as nature, it would not necessarily follow that it is of any particular human colour. In the iconography of British imperialism, nature has often been black or brown. But we know anyway that much of the countryside we seek is not nature. It is not a space of nature to which we retreat from human society. It is a very particular kind of social space, created by human labour and shaped by social relations over many centuries. However much we might fall into a discourse of unspoilt nature, in many cases our appreciation of the British countryside is clearly not a delight in wilderness: it rests very much on our implicit knowledge of its having been socially created.[4] Moreover, it has been created through the labour of human bodies which have to an overwhelming degree historically been white. There are no doubt examples from the past and present of black farm workers in Britain. But such people are so few in number that all our images of the workers on the land are of white workers. The dozen men we see standing around the hayrick in the Victorian photograph, the carters, ploughmen, woodmen, shepherds and dairymen we have met in photographs and illustrations and stories, and who populate our imaginary visions of the country, are all white, as are the women of field and farm.

The argument requires a further step, however, because it may not be seen to follow necessarily from our awareness of the whiteness of centuries of agricultural labourers that we experience the countryside itself as white. The further step we must take concerns the nature of primary process, which is the name Freud gave to the most basic and primitive level of mental functioning. Psychoanalysis and anthropology converge on the insight that our most modern states of mind co-exist with forms of irrationality and magical thought, one of which is based on the principle of contagion. According to J.G. Frazer (1911, p. 52) this principle (observed by him to be active in many European rural communities in the early years of this century) determines that 'things which have once been in contact with each other continue to act on each other at a distance after the physical contact has been severed'. It means that things once close to each other acquire a sameness of identity or spirit. Blood on the weapon continues in sympathy with that in the injured one's body; what is done to an object against which someone has been accidentally injured will affect the healing of the wound. The fate of nail-clippings and teeth, or of the placenta, will affect the fate of the individual to whom they were once connected.

Most of Frazer's examples are of attempts to bring either benefit or harm to individuals by appropriate treatment of something once close to or part of them, that is, they belong to the social practice of magic, and they do not in themselves justify the suggestion being made here, which seeks to postulate a contemporary pattern of feeling and to attribute it to the principle of contagion. The feeling is that if the bodies which have laboured on the land, shaped it and sweated into it have been white, then – at some level of collective phantasy – so must the body of the land itself be white. In his discussion of Frazer, Freud (1913, pp. 81ff.) not surprisingly stresses the importance of the *wish* in the dynamics of the magic – the connection is believed to exist because it is wished for (or feared). So perhaps in the present analysis we need also to imagine a sort of ideological input to the phantasy – a wish that Britain were still white (and the fear that in its heart it is).[5]

Additionally, or perhaps as an expression of the primitive deduction that the past togetherness of phenomena causes a present sympathy between them, there is a traditional notion that we are all somehow constituted materially by the earth on which we stand, that we spring from the earth. This belief has obviously had its strongest expression in nationalistic and fascistic ideologies of blood and soil, but is present in non-pathological and much broader cultural traditions, for example in the notion that we progress from ashes to ashes, and from dust to dust.

So there is in our collective phantasies a cycle of reciprocal reproduction involving land and humanity. In the subliminal imagination of the culture, the human bodies both issue from and create the earthly body on which they walk. And if the bodies are white, the land from which they rise and on which they lay is also white. So the long history of agricultural labour by white labourers upon the British countryside, a history of which everyone is to some degree apprised, orients us to an experience of the countryside itself as a white body. It is not really relevant at this level of experience to point out that it was the labour of black slaves in the West Indies, and of peoples in the Indian sub-continent, that provided some of the wealth that shaped the British landscape as a place of comfort and order. It is not relevant because unconscious phantasy is not constrained by historical truth. It draws upon experience of the external world, but British imperialism did not make the brute facts of slavery a central datum of experience for the Britsh people.

We can add to this argument a consideration not only of labour on the surface of the landscape, but also of labour beneath or within it. As we look across the land of many parts of Britain, we know that there exist elaborate creations of human labour beneath these surfaces, in the mines. Human labour has worked not only on the fair face of the land but also in its bowels.[6] At the height of the coal industry, almost as many men worked underground as there are now people employed by the British National Health Service, said to be the largest employer in Europe. There might be a useful comparison here, which goes beyond the immediate concerns of this chapter though it is still oriented to the central place of phantasies about the body in the formation of personal and national identities.

For many people, the NHS is central to their more optimistic visions of what kind of nation Britain is, or could be. It is a vision organised around the centrality in human life of illness and pain, and around the importance of protecting all people in the nation from, and supporting them in their struggles with, disease and disability. It is also a vision of multiraciality, since almost from its inception the NHS has been a multiracial institution. Hence much of its positive symbolic value in political discourse, whatever its actual shortcomings. It presents to us an image of the national body which is vulnerable to suffering but which can be healed or comforted through an inclusive, multiracial social institution based on values of care and expertise.

Not long ago, though, the mining industry occupied a similarly central space in the national consciousness, and played an equally prominent part in defining what kind of nation Britain was: one based on small industrial communities and the values of working-class solidarity, continuity and a masculine ethos of manual labour. The body of this nation was being created beneath the fields and moors. Again, especially in recent years, there have been black miners, but the great weight of our documentary and imaginary images of the miner calls up for us the picture of the white man, turned black by his labours perhaps, but himself as white as the coal is black. And it is the white bodies of generations of miners who have a place in our shared phantasies of what the body of the British nation is made of and who have helped to create the actual landscape of the countryside with their pitheads and slag-heaps.

The implication of this general line of analysis is that if a black person feels some sense of not quite belonging, however obscure that sense might be, it is not only because the countryside is today actually populated and used mainly by white people. It is also because – to adapt a famous line from Marx – the dead weight of the past lies in the minds of the living. Specifically, the bodies of the dead fill the minds of the living. And perhaps there is no more direct statement of the whiteness of the rural body in which an important part of the British national identity resides than the country churchyard, where we can be confident that all the bodies over which we tread and whose tissue has merged with the earth are white.

There is another quality to our projections onto the country-side which has not yet been mentioned, one which is linked to our experience of it as a white body but which is separable from it. This is the idealisation of the country as a pure and clean and

wholesome body, as the embodiment of healing nature. When
the two phantasies are fused, we have a racist vision of the
British countryside at the heart of a white purity and goodness.
And although the two are not necessarily fused, the extent to
which both are embedded in our traditions suggests that here
may be an important unconscious (but contingent) source of
racism – the co-option into the racist mind-set of universal
images of gentle and healing nature.

In any case, psychoanalytic thinking expects that where
there is idealisation there is a corresponding denigration of
something else. In the case of the idealisation of the country,
this is the body of the city as the site of danger and dirt, as a
suffocating environment, a fragmented and bizarre place, and
so on. Specifically, the inner city has come to carry the most
virulent material in this projective field, such that it is seen as
the site of growth of the most malignant tumours which can
form within the body of the nation.

It seems that this is an example of how the deployment of
unconscious phantasies can be channelled by actual historical
processes, and that the inner city has been set up by social
change to function as a 'bad object' for us in our unconscious
as well as conscious minds. These are the socio-economic
processes which have involved the de-industrialisation and
selective de-population of inner urban areas, the deterioration
of their housing stock and – particularly – the changes in the
ethnic composition of their populations. Given the old imperi-
alist and racist traditions of associating blackness with dirt,
this latter demographic change would have facilitated the
unconscious registration of the inner city as a place of dirt
and badness.

Positive feedback loops are then set up, with phantasies
about the body of the city and about the bodies of its black
and brown residents reinforcing each other. Images of damage
and defectiveness have come to complement ones of dirt,
such that the damaged and diseased body of the inner city is
felt to produce diseased and damaged people. Their only
relationship to the countryside would be like that of slum
children taken out into it for a Whitsun Treat, or of nine-
teenth-century East End children taken to Hampstead Heath
at weekends by settlement workers for the fresh air, but
whose place in the country could never be more than
temporary, medicinal and exceptional.

Of course, actual experience of the city may result in very

different patterns of feeling about it. Bruno Bettelheim (1990), writing about the sense of home, describes how his early experience of Vienna (and its place in his family's history) established the city for him as, in general, a good and providing place. Yet there can be no doubting the wide currency of strongly negative phantasies about the city, as the complement to the idealisation of the rural environment.

LOSS AND DISCOVERY

The burden of the argument so far in this chapter is not very optimistic, since it suggests that the exclusion of many people from the pleasures of the countryside is not all that amenable to modification by simple changes in practices, by more coach trips to North Wales for the Muslim women of the Midlands, valuable though such may be. Where primitive phantasy is involved, the realignment of feelings may not be a straightforward matter. But phantasies can be contained, and they can also be deployed to a potentially infinite variety of different social ends. Also we should bear in mind why the countryside, however much it may be the object of racially-exclusive phantasies, is also a source of solace and regeneration for so many of us.

This is to return to the other side of the contradiction from which the chapter began. Psychoanalytically thinking, this restorative function of the countryside is in part because we find there an image of a lost object. For much contemporary psychoanalytic thinking, the experience of loss is at the centre of emotional development. The earliest and most fundamental loss is that of the mother, and of the relationship which the baby has with the mother. In the early experience of everyone there is an image of an enfolding, loving and nurturant mother, whether or not this image was consistently matched by external reality – it is basically a phantasy, deriving from the baby's *need* for nurturance and from its projected omnipotence. Emotional development is based on the individual being able to confront the loss of this primal object, and to develop an emotional independence from it. In Freud's terms, it centres on the development of the capacity to live by the reality principle, to tolerate the reality of loss. In the Kleinian development of Freud's theory, this task is complicated by the need to confront also the baby's fear that in greed and anger it may have damaged the good object. This 'depressive anxiety' is the basis of the experience of guilt, and of efforts to make amends to or repair the damaged object, both internally and in the external world.

The countryside is one of the most powerful repositories in British culture of the sense of loss. Hence the magnificent melancholy of the music of Elgar and the other pastoralists of modern British music. This sense of loss is subject to a range of different inflections, but common to most of them is the feeling that the countryside has been irrevocably damaged by the forces of social change. This lament does not apply only to the countryside, of course, and we may suspect that the impersonal evil of social 'progress' stands here as a metaphor for personal maturation. While we are all the beneficiaries of emotional development (as we are of many socio-technological developments), we are very ambivalent about it (as we are about social change). The rigidities and inhibitions that allegedly come with age are derided, the lost innocence and spontaneity of earlier years are mourned. Collective nostalgia for the lost countryside may be fed in part by nostalgia for what each individual has lost in the course of growing up, especially in the earliest and most basic stages, with separation from the mother's body and person.

In the case of the countryside, the loss is of course the historical *fantasy* of a beauty, purity and innocence that once existed in some earlier day. It is not in any simple sense an actual historical loss. But in partaking of this historical fantasy, we enable ourselves to work through feelings of loss, and to feel that we confront in the countryside the traces of a precious and nurturant object from which we have been separated, and which we fear we have harmed. The experience can be tantalising or mournful, but also restorative and integrative, to the extent that we can feel that we have rediscovered and internalised the good object. Some calm images of hill and stream, elements of a soothing 'environment mother', to use Winnicott's phrase, may as a consequence be felt to reside more securely inside us. Although we cannot undo the social changes that have modified, and in some places destroyed, the countryside, we can reassure ourselves that it is still there, still able to offer some goodness.

This argument would suggest that participation in such 'depressive' working through is readily available only to those who can identify with the historical image of the countryside as a white body. Now it may be that the experience of melancholic yearning for a lost arcadia is so universal and powerful a component of modern experience that people of different colours and cultures can use many kinds of rural landscape to plug directly into it. It may be though that this is not the case, and that if you yearn for the Malverns or the hills of Northern Pakistan, then the Pyrenees, though they can be appreciated, will fundamentally not do. So we probably cannot unite in diversity around the countryside as an object of commemorative experience.

There is however another way of thinking about the experience of the countryside which may hold out some prospects for reworking and extending our cultural imagery in a way that is based on ethnic diversity and inclusiveness. We can take some encouragement as to the possibility of this from the development of association football, as discussed in the previous chapter. Football has also been vital to the British self-consciousness, and race has also been a key issue for it in recent years. The body of the footballer, and of the sport as a whole, was for most of its history in Britain a white one. Consequently the first black players in the English League in the 1950s and 1960s had a very difficult time. For many people, the black body simply did not quite belong at the centre of the game. But in a relatively short period, thanks to the skills of the now numerous black players and to other changes at work within the sport, football – and the powerful feelings and phantasies linked with it – have been substantially de-racialised and internationalised. It was suggested in Chapter 3 that racial and national diversity are now becoming contained within the British game instead of marking its boundaries. It still needs more professional Asian players, and there is still racism in the stands, but very significant progress has been made. The cultural markings of race have been radically re-drawn in a crucial sector of popular experience.

There is an important parallel we can draw between the appeal of football and that of the countryside, and to do so will help to elaborate the general perspective on popular culture which this book adopts. In both cases there is a combination of sensuality with social restraint. While each of these dimensions is essential to the experience of enjoyment, it is the social discipline which must predominate if the enjoyment is to remain secure and attractive on a mass scale. As was noted, social discipline in football is expressed basically in the rules of the game. In our appreciation of the countryside, the social is displayed in the lines laid across it by centuries of labour – in the hedgerows, lanes, ditches and so on – and in the general sense of order and domestication imposed upon the swelling plenitude of the earth.

That we remain gladly bound to the social and its disciplines, even in the midst of our escape to the pastoral, is suggested by the practice of greeting any stranger one happens to see on a walk,[7] though this is probably primarily a nostalgic reference to the lost village community. Generally, our delight in the countryside – whether as walkers in it or as consumers of images of it – draws on the sense of relief and euphoria in the discovery that we are enfolded by a social world, which offers up to us powerful sensual pleasures but reassures us that civil life is firmly established around us, restraining and protective.

We are working here with a version of Freud's theory of culture, which sees it as the successful struggle of rational ego over libidinal id, but one in which the libidinal truth of experience must not be lost if the cultural artefact or practice is to retain its hold on us. It has also been argued that at the centre of our experience of the countryside is the feeling that it represents something that is lost. In this way also it confronts one who encounters it with the comforting fact of one's social membership, of which the loss of the infantile state is the price. Although this sense of loss is a powerful psychic reality, it is illusory if translated directly into external reality, and the revered object symbolising the lost mother is felt to have been *really* lost. This is the psychic basis for fascist fantasies of retrieving the motherland. But in reality, those who enter the countryside are often discovering it rather than seeking to reclaim it. Many of today's walking classes are the first in their families to appropriate it as a source of pleasure, and it is increasingly the object of an institutionalised leisure activity for day-trippers. In the course of this century the development of transport systems has delivered the countryside to ever wider numbers of people, though of course changing large parts of it in the process. As an intensively managed leisure resource, the countryside is a relatively new kind of social space, rather like the shopping mall, and is therefore available to be defined in new ways.

While it will remain closely linked to very strong traditions of feeling, and the imagery associated with it will change slowly, we – especially the non-white we – can hope to do more with it, in our imaginations as well as in our leisure time, than we have been able to do previously. Changes in practice can lead to changes in imagery and phantasy content.

5 THE GREAT CAR SOCIETY

TECHNOPHOBIA AND TECHNOPHILIA

There is again but a short step to the subject of our next case study,[1] via a contrast. The motor car is often seen as the antithesis of the countryside and the values it represents for us, and as the main cause of its feared disappearance. If we can identify in relation to the motor car some of the same themes which have emerged in the previous discussion of pastoral imagery, it would suggest there are some strongly unifying forces at work in popular culture, some psychosocial processes which may cut across, or lie beneath, its undeniably increasing diversity. One possible link between the discourses of the countryside and of the car swiftly suggests itself. The one is part of the discourse of nature, and the other part of the discourse of technology, and in many influential traditions of thought and feeling nature and technology are tied together, albeit usually as opposites. But whereas the forms of 'nature' available in a country such as Britain are typically seen in positive terms only, there is a much more obvious ambivalence about 'technology'.

By drawing on psychoanalytic thinking, which has a lot to say about ambivalence, it is possible to make some useful observations on the discourse of technology. The motor car, which both in material and symbolic terms is fundamental to popular culture, will be our example, though some of the observations to be made may also apply to the understanding of attitudes towards other forms of technology such as information and medical technologies.

Any discussion of the motor car today, even if oriented primarily towards the understanding of popular culture, is also inevitably a contribution to debates about the environment. There may indeed be some hopes here for a marriage of psychoanalytic insight with environmentalist politics. This relationship cannot however be a completely harmonious one, and the blame for this lies in a sense with psychoanalysis.

Psychoanalysis is a relentlessly critical character. As we know, it refuses to take what people say at face value, and is constantly probing for a reality which is more complex and usually less congenial than is at first apparent. Because of its unyielding nature, psychoanalysis has had some failed relationships in the past with suitors from the world of politics. Some of us at one time held out great hopes for its relationship with Marxism. But, although they had some good times together, that liaison ran aground against the refusal of psychoanalysis to exempt anything from its analytic gaze, not least the murky unconscious of the revolutionary.

Nonetheless, I do not want to warn environmentalism off from an involvement with psychoanalysis. Difficult though it may be, it has a great deal to offer to someone who can take criticism. So while we may prefer it when psychoanalysis is laying bear the unconscious dynamics which threaten the planetary ecology, for example by locating the origins of environmental vandalism in attacks upon the mother, which is surely an important line of enquiry, we also have to listen carefully when the phantasies and anxieties that help to drive the environmentalist are also explored. So, for example, we may question the possible role in ecological concern of phantasies of a depleted and retaliating mother, of a vengeful mother smothering us (the greenhouse effect), or of a damaged mother unable to protect us from harmful impingement (ozone depletion). In other words we can turn to psychoanalysis not only for some insights into why environmentalist goals and priorities are so widely rejected in practice by so many people, but also for some insights into how some of those goals and priorities may themselves be infused with irrational and defensive processes. And psychoanalysis for its part must take its place in the array of disciplines which can be deployed within environmental politics.

The terms technophilia and technophobia will be used as a way of highlighting how technologies evoke in us strong positive and negative feelings which impede rational discussion of them, and which produce reverential or dismissive attitudes rather than realistic appraisal of their social and environmental costs and benefits. Taken together these terms emphasise that there is more than one way of being irrational about technology. In the context of some present-day 'green' rhetoric it may sometimes seem as if there is only one kind of problem, namely our over-valuation of technologies even though they may be highly destructive of the environment. In some cases, this kind of attitude may be appropriately described as 'technophilic', in that it may issue from a phantasy in which technology is an idealised object endowed with magical powers, and with which the individual may be narcissistically identified. The existence of this kind of state of mind is clearly a major obstacle to the development of ecological sanity, since the environmental costs of the technology will be denied or scorned. Psychoanalytic explorations of this problem have played a part in clarifying and widening our awareness of it, particularly in its most dangerous manifestations in the nuclear age (see, e.g. Easlea, 1983, among many writings of the 1980s on military technophilia).

This is probably the kind of progeny which some might have hoped would issue from the marriage of psychoanalysis and environmentalism. But there is another kind of problem to which psychoanalysis will, in its even-handedness, also wish to draw attention. This is one which environmentalists are more likely to find in their own minds than in those of the others whom they seek to persuade or oppose. This is the problem of technophobia, or irrational fear of technology, as manifested in prejudiced condemnations of it, self-denying avoidance or rejection of particular forms of it, and a general loss of grip on the reality of the technology and its powers and effects. Many of us have experienced at least mild forms of technophobia in the first stages of our encounter with information technology.

CAR BODIES

Arguably the most important of modern technologies is that embodied in the motor car – important in the sense of the global size of the motor industry and its dependent trades, and in respect of the social and cultural changes facilitated or imposed on us by the spread of car use. It is well-known that the car, since its appearance at the end of the last century, has been the object of technophilic feeling, which may indeed have contributed to the extent to which the car has become the dominant material object in many present-day environments.

The affection in which men in particular are believed to hold their cars is an established source of amusement. The fascination of some young males with cars has become a subject of serious social concern in response to the statistics showing large increases in car-related crime, and to the part played by exhibitionistic driving of stolen vehicles in some recent social disturbances. And of course a selfish passion for cars is not confined to the criminal margins. Since General Motors introduced annual model changes and styling extravagance in the 1930s, the car has for many groups in society been the most conspicuous item of conspicuous consumption, of social display. And in some popular images of it, the car has gone beyond this mere assertion of social status to represent the means of escape from society, the transcendence of the mass through style and mobility.

At first sight, it may seem as if psychoanalysis has provided clichés rather than insights into the meanings of the car. Yet beneath the clichés a truth remains. Cars are about sexuality. There are of course the clichéd propositions that the car is a phallic object, and in some contexts such clichés are no doubt true, but this is only one of a plethora of conscious and unconscious sexual meanings which are elaborated around the car. The phenomenon of fuel 'injection' is one example of this. Until the mid-1980s, this was normally found only in sportier models. The sexual connotations of this technology, and the terms used to describe it, were important in establishing it as a desirable feature. (Images of copulating rabbits and rhinos were sometimes found on the rear ends of some Volkswagens and Suzukis with 'injection'.) And there is more to it than the car-as-phallus; the car injects itself, the whole intercourse is on wheels. The car is both male body, punching its way through the traffic, and also graceful female body. It is at once sexual instrument, object and act. In phantasy, as registered so clearly by some advertisements, we may endow it with all the hope which, at the deepest levels of feeling, surrounds the procreative couple.[2]

While it may be true, at one important level, that images of the sexual couple and of a happy family life are used to sell cars (i.e. that advertisements plunder these other meanings to attach them to cars), we cannot assume that marketing alone creates the full depth of signification which cars have. It may be that the readiness with which we surround the car with the auras of sexuality and family life owes something to its intrinsic properties. The car embodies two of the basic figures of hope in modern society: sexuality (perhaps, through its meanings as reproduction, the basic figure of hope in any society), and – as will shortly be argued – autonomy. These figures flag the developmental paths along which individuals move, and hope – in its broadest, existential sense – depends on the feeling that enough progress has been, or can be, made along them.

The sceptic would say that such 'fanciful' analyses of unconscious phantasy are unnecessary to explain the appeal of a technology like fuel injection, which in reality gives more efficiency and power for the same engine capacity. But it is hard to maintain that car buying is predominantly governed by rational considerations. If it were, safety features would not need to be promoted so heavily, often via advertisements which address more than realistic concerns about accidents, and tap also into wishes for enduring family harmony, and into phantasies of invulnerability.

The phrase 'moving metal', meaning the selling of cars, is a clue to another of the automobile's attractions. The particular magic of cars is sometimes felt to lie in the combination they present of raw animal and refined metal, human qualities of movement and vigour fused with superhuman technology. While one of its competitors is the 'big cat' (Jaguar), the BMW is 'the ultimate driving *machine*': the inhuman power of the metal machine is the ultimate transcendence of the mortal limits of ordinary bodies. Both inflections posit the car as a new, awesome kind of supernatural object.

Mercedes too trades on its machine-like qualities, suggesting to us another cultural dimension of car imagery. Stereotypical images of nations are at work in the car market – the mechanical might of the Germans, the stylish sensuality of the Italians, the fashionable individuality of the French, and so on. The experience of nationhood, and of other nations, has – as was discussed in the previous chapter – always been deeply linked with images of the body. Whether admiring, fearful or contemptuous (for example the general mirth just before the reunification of Germany over the rudimentary Trabant cars of the East, and other attitudes towards East European cars), these images link the body, the nation and the car in patterns that strongly influence car sales.

Like the nation, the car provides a living space. In the public world of outdoors it creates a space around the body which is almost as inviolable as the body itself. And within this space there is a maternal administration to the physical comfort of the occupants. Increasingly car interiors strive to create a universe of perfect accommodation – in layout, texture, sound and temperature – to every need of the occupant's body. Inside the rigid cage of safety there is a soft, uterine environment to nurture the driver through the journey. As Isabel Menzies-Lyth (1989) established in market research in the 1960s, the car is as much a protective maternal body as it is a thrusting male one. It creates a private space within public space, a safe zone within which there is a maternal administration to the comfort of the occupants.

The car is a particularly appropriate 'vehicle' for these and other projections because it is or has a body, which can hold and contain us, and which moves. It is a large moving object which we can enter and control, and it has a sort of metabolism and creates waste products (of particular relevance to us today). It suffers from a variety of ailments and breakdowns, and it ages quite visibly. There are not many objects which can invite us so directly to experience them in somatomorphic ways, that is to exercise to the full our tendency to experience things as if they were bodies. So we project onto the car a rich variety of meanings derived from bodily experience. We can experience the car as both a male and female body; the driver may experience the car either as sexual partner or as extension of his or her own body. The car offers a collection of surfaces and shapes which may be deployed within a very wide range of libidinal scenarios. As will be pointed out a little further on, not all of these endow it with positive meanings. The phallus can be feared and hated as well as glorified; the mother can be terrifying. But for the moment let us stick with technophilia.

Perhaps the most helpful general formulation we can make about technophilia in relation to the car, and probably some other technologies as well, is in terms of narcissism. Psychoanalytically speaking, this means not so much a love of one's body or oneself as a phantasy of perfection that can be projected onto all sorts of things. The car is revered because it is experienced as the embodiment of a narcissistic phantasy: it is then felt to have magical properties. Its power and its sensuous qualities will be narcissistically over-valued; in identifying with it the driver will feel omnipotent. We can see the clearest signs of this technophilic state of mind in car advertisements and their invitations to omnipotence and transcendence. We must be careful here, however, since it is a common failing of much social criticism to believe what it sees in advertisements, that is to assume that adverts exhaustively define our relationships to goods. While they are certainly an influence, we know from our own experience that goods can have all sorts of different meanings for us, which are at most partially apprehended in the advertisements. Nonetheless it is reasonable to propose that many of the meanings associated with the car are of a technophilic kind, consisting as they do of images of ideal bodies, impregnable havens, mythical excitements, perfect machines, and so on.

FREE TO MOVE

Another source of adulation of the motor vehicle is grounded in its reality not just as a physical object with certain sensual properties, but as a means of transport. This basic functionality of the car (getting from A to B) is not simply a matter of its practical effectiveness, since our experience of such practicalities is inevitably infused with unconscious meaning.

The car is deeply linked with the experience of individual freedom, so much so that it is hard to imagine any significantly wide social movement to renounce it. This is not an easy fact to grasp. We are accustomed to think of freedom in terms of political conditions, of civil rights, the media, artistic expression and so on. The suggestion that a material commodity, least of all the vulgar car, can in itself be a source of freedom is inimical to much of our thinking. In today's more technophobic climate, we are accustomed to seeing the car in terms of selfish individualism and conspicuous consumption, and the idea that something as clearly destructive of natural resources as it has been could also have a realistically positive side is psychologically a difficult one to take on board. We tend to want things to be either good or bad, not powerful mixtures of the two.

Yet at the same time we are also familiar with the idea that consumer goods can enhance life, and not only in the direction of individualistic hedonism. In the case of the telephone, for example, a high-technology individual possession creates many possibilities for interpersonal contact to enrich relationships or remove anxieties; it enhances the freedom of remote and less mobile individuals to participate in personal relationships and in social activity. If telephone use was destroying the ozone layer, it seems more likely that we would be trying to find ozone-friendly telephones, rather than to attack or minimise telephone use.

Two major reasons can be proposed for why the car is profoundly associated with freedom. One is based in the development of the individual, and one in the development of modern society. They are two aspects of a deep psychic connection between freedom and movement – not movement *per se*, but personally willed and executed movement. As the baby and toddler separates itself psychologically from those who care for it, its ability and freedom to move away – and to come back – are of enormous significance to it. To set off, to move, to arrive, to turn around, to change direction, to vary one's pace – these are all important elements in the experience of separating out, of establishing the autonomy and agency of the developing individual.

These are the experiences which driving a car can daily reconfirm, as we re-enact the pleasures of locomotion in a technologically transformed way. A little later in childhood, not just the sheer fact of movement but the sense of sure-footed, swift and poised movement enters importantly into psychological development. Driving can recreate in an adult world these pleasures of successful locomotion, and can confirm and enhance the sense of achievement and autonomy gained from our earliest journeys. (As another Rover ad has said, underneath pictures of a toddler walking and in a pedal car, a small boy on a bike and a young man in his first car, 'Life's journeys should be unforgettable'.)

The design of cars has increasingly oriented itself towards this developmentally important aesthetics of movement. In adolescence, the discourse of autonomy often becomes focused upon geographical mobility (getting away from home), and also becomes fully sexualised, which greatly enlarges its aesthetic possibilities. The car, then, taps into powerful sources of feeling at all these developmental levels, and not just to revive for the adult some of the pleasures of earlier development, but to redeploy on an adult scale the feelings associated with the achievement of mobility.

In our adult relationships to others, and to our society, space and distance remain crucial variables. Historically, to be free has been in large part to be free to move. Freedom of movement is one of the most obvious contrasts between the slavery and serfdom of precapitalist forms of society, and the wage labour of capitalism. And within the period of capitalist development, increasing freedom of movement has become emblematic of increased personal freedom generally. Of course the car is not the only vehicle of this mobility, as some popular images of the Greyhound Bus, the motor-bike and the aeroplane make clear. The personal car is however its most powerful expression and most complete means. It is probably no accident that advanced capitalism has produced, as its leading commodity, an object which so closely matches and enhances one of its most striking achievements – the aspiration, and the opportunity, to move freely around the country with all the possibilities for individual fulfilment and for contact with others which that brings.

The powerful appeal of the car is based therefore not only on a sensual aesthetic, upon the aptness of the vehicle for representing many of our feelings about and wishes for our bodies. It is not only about the car as sexual. It is also based on the aptness of the car for the expression and consummation of some of the deepest aspects of modern individuality, of our development as psychologically separate persons in a world of social mobility and of individual rights. It matters not to the depth of our wishes for mobility that the freedom to move has for millions of people across history meant mainly that they suffer in a different place. Whether as an imaginary or real benefit, the freedom to move is of real psychological importance.

When the wish for individualised freedom to move is compounded with practical difficulties in getting to places within specified times by public transport, then there are very strong forces combining to put more cars on the road. But again, our feelings about public transport are not based only on practical considerations of reliability, frequency, cost and so on. Even the best public transport system does not provide the experience of agency and autonomy available to the driver and passengers of a private car. Whatever else they may have to put up with in the felt and hidden costs of traffic jams, the stresses of driving and so on, they are spared the anxieties of missing the bus or train (which can activate much deeper unconscious fears of abandonment). They can preserve around themselves a truly personal space, with no fear of intruding on others with their conversation or music, and they can vary or interrupt their journeys at will.

If the movement to reduce the ecological damage done by

the car ignores these psychological benefits, or writes them off as unnecessary expressions of an unwholesome individualism, it will be failing to understand the problem we face. There is little hope of substantially limiting the use of cars by anything less than highly coercive measures, which would be politically unwelcome and unstable. What we can expect is an inevitable escalation of global car production and use as the pleasures and benefits of the car are claimed by more people, especially in those countries where the levels of car ownership are at present low. This is not to say that measures to minimise the use that people make of their cars by improving public transport should not be given full support (not least because a good public system is owed to those without cars). It does however suggest that any strategy for ecological salvation which wants to respect the reality and validity of modern desires must focus upon the reduction of waste and pollution caused by motor vehicles rather than upon curbing the spread of the car.

EXCURSION INTO POLICY

A number of the analyses offered in this book could be oriented towards practical questions of policy, in quite diverse areas such as the arts and their support, the regulation of advertising and conservationist strategies. At this point, since some policy questions concerning the motor car and transport choices are within particularly close reach of the present discussion, we will briefly pursue one of them, namely the issue of how motor vehicles are powered. This will enable us to see how psychoanalytically influenced thinking might fit into areas of debate which are quite remote from its traditional concerns.

To begin with, two complementary myths must be disposed of (with implications for many other fields as well as transport). The first is that popular desires are entirely manufactured by those who stand to profit from them. It has been argued that in the case of consumer demand for cars, this is not so; the roots are much deeper than that, as they are in other areas of mass consumption and popular culture. The second is that popular desires are virtually immune to the blandishments and pressures of advertising and publicity, that consumers are headstrong creatures who know what their wants are and don't pay any attention to attempts to influence them. Both of these false assumptions turn up frequently in debates about the politics of consumption.

Thus it has been claimed that the American public does not like diesel engines, and that there is no point therefore in trying to make and market diesels for the American car buyer. It may well be true that American motorists have tended to think negatively of diesels; it certainly is not true that this is an immutable fact of life. The conversion of British motorists to lead-free petrol was visibly generated by a combination of tax differentials and vigorous marketing, against the grain of some received meanings according to which lead was very desirable in petrol (linked to the idea of lead as a toughening element, as in 'put some lead in his pencil'). These fiscal and marketing changes were in turn driven by an upcoming EC requirement for catalytic converters, which can only use unleaded. The development of concern with 'green' issues has created a favourable basis for the increased use of all pollution-reducing devices, but in this case as in others it was research and development, and then crucially marketing and tax policy, which actually secured a change in practice. (Since, it has been suggested that unleaded petrol is a mixed blessing in health terms, but that is another issue.)

If the American consumer had been seen as a more tractable creature, some of the enormous resources which have gone into the development of the catalytic converter, to satisfy what was taken to be the American need for a clean petrol engine, might have gone into the development of diesel technology. Diesel engines have been seen from one environmentalist position as the least of all evils at the moment, since (as well as being lead-free) they have much lower fuel consumption and thereby produce much less carbon dioxide per vehicle mile.

Again, recent evidence has produced a further twist in the arguments, with indications that diesel emissions may be more carcinogenic than was thought. But the spread of diesel engines has been limited more by their problematic nature in marketing terms: the trouble is that they have not been 'sexy', to put it in the manner of marketing's rough approximation to psychological truth. Yet intercooler and direct-injection technology can produce turbodiesel cars which match most petrol models in performance, and advocates of diesel have suggested that with investment to produce further progress in tackling the problems of noise, vibration and particulate emission, and with the right marketing, the diesel could be rendered highly desirable. The increasing production of diesel models with 'sports' specification in body styling and accessories indicates the current fluidity of meanings here, and following the argument of this chapter, body styling has a paramount role within the sphere of desire-led car purchase.

The unattractiveness of diesels is therefore highly contingent upon the uses made by marketing of the wide range of meanings linked with engine technologies. Ironically, the readiness to vary these meanings is growing at the moment when the environmental benefits of diesel are more sharply questioned than before. In any case, within the sphere of environmental and economic rationalities, the diesel car is only one of several possible means to lower pollution and running costs. The first production battery-powered car will soon be with us. And there is two-stroke technology, another way of making worthwhile savings in fuel use. The key point is that governments can choose which path to take, and that within limits consumer demand can be engineered to fit the chosen path of technological development. The most basic limits are given by the unlikelihood – for the reasons set out in this chapter – of the demand for individualised means of transport disappearing.

There are two prerequisites for effectively choosing whatever might be the ecologically optimal ways of powering personal vehicles. These are a government commitment to support them with appropriate taxation policies, and a commitment by the motor industry to engineering those choices, both technologically and socially. This strategy, unlike the green abolitionist one, would accept the powerful needs for autonomy which the car meets, rather than trying to wish them away. It would aim to deploy the images of freedom and sensuality with which cars are traditionally associated in a new way, linking them to ecological sensibilities and to radically revised technologies. We cannot hope to stop the spread of the car; we can hope to drive cars that are minimally polluting, substantially recyclable and manufactured in ecologically responsible ways. The skills and resources normally available in the design and marketing of motor cars should be more than adequate to achieving this.

THE MAKING OF A BAD OBJECT

The car has brought to millions the kind of personal mobility and autonomy available at the start of this century only to a privileged few. It has enabled people to have much greater choice in the labour market, it has been the basis for a restructuring of the retail industry in ways that most people experience as more convenient and enabling, it has opened up many new forms and locations of leisure, and it has given people more freedom in the building of social networks and personal relationships.

Against this background, the technophobic experience of the car clearly requires some explanation. It is quite striking how in the course of the last decade or so the car has become such a bad object in public discourse. A number of different forces have been working towards this end: the growing concern with safety in all walks of life, and the consequent concern with death and injury on the roads; the feminist critique of technology and its frequent implication that the car is typically a boy's toy; and the relative erosion or dilapidation of public transport systems, which has brought to the fore the idea that there are societal choices to be made between different forms of transport, choices which were obscured while public transport was continuing to expand alongside the growth in car use, as was the case until relatively recently. And most importantly, of course, there has been the rise of environmentalist concerns about the pollution costs of various forms of transport. The belief that the car is a poisonous object has fixed it in our minds as a major source of badness in the contemporary material world.

There is no doubt that lead in petrol was responsible for a slow form of poisoning suffered by some urban dwellers in recent decades. That problem was substantially solved by the introduction of unleaded petrol, though the survival of many older cars that do not function well on it has limited the implementation of the solution, and unleaded petrol also burns less completely, leaving higher quantities of other substances in the air. The catalytic converter provides a way of dealing to some extent with most other toxic emissions, with the exception of carbon dioxide. Here for many people is the nub of the problem. CO_2 is the main greenhouse gas, and is inevitably produced by the burning of any fossil fuel (and

notably the use of 'cats' slightly increases the output of CO_2).
The recent advances in emission control, plus other improvements in engineering technology and car design, have meant
that emission levels other than CO_2 are now falling, despite
the global growth in vehicle use (Walsh, 1990) but as the
number of vehicles worldwide continues to rise they will start
to climb again in the next century unless there are further
technological or statutory changes (which of course is not
impossible). Meanwhile CO_2 output from the roads continues
to rise, though it could be reduced by a mass switch to diesel
or perhaps two-stroke engines.

There are however now technological possibilities for almost pollution-free engines, using 'biodiesel'. A form of this
based on rape-seed oil is already available in a number of
European countries, and can be used by diesel engines
without modification. In the production and use cycles of any
vegetable-based fuel, there is no net increase in CO_2. It is
also relevant to note that the contribution of CO_2 to the
so-called greenhouse gases is about 50 per cent, and that the
contribution of vehicles to total CO_2 output is about 20 per
cent. So we are talking about 10 per cent of the greenhouse
problem. That is, of course, if you believe there is a greenhouse problem, which – as Simon Hoggart of *The Observer* has
been fond of reminding us – is a contested hypothesis. If
there is such a problem, the major sources of it are to be
found in the energy-consuming infrastructures of modern life,
but these are less easily objected to by the environmentalist
than the discrete and individualised mode of transport.

These technical arguments are relevant here because they
put the extreme animosity which exists towards the car in a
context which does not obviously justify it. Serious though
automobile polluting effects have been and may still be, they
are arguably not a massive threat to the planetary ecology,
and are in any case not entirely intrinsic to the car as such.

So we might ask if there are any other reasons why the car
in essence is so deeply experienced as a bad, noxious object.
It can be suggested firstly that a large measure of the hostility
towards the motor car is not so much ecological in the narrow
biological sense, but more aesthetic and social. People do not
like the ubiquity of cars with their noise and bulk and the
clamour of their occupants. These are environmental effects,
of course, in that they concern the quality of the environment,
but they are part of the environment as a socio-aesthetic

space rather than as a biophysical system. Also, they concern the car *en masse*, cars in the multitude rather than the solitary vehicle. Though there are some people who find any car at best an uninteresting lump of metal and plastic, there is a wide recognition that the individual car can be an object of great aesthetic interest. Yet there is a difference between standing in the Design Museum admiring individual examples of the VW Beetle or Toyota Previa as metallic sculptures, and standing waiting to cross the road as countless VWs, Toyotas and what have you stream past in their brute metallic otherness.

In other words, the problem of the car is that there are so many of them. The problem is that the car is an object of *mass* consumption and use. The tirade against the car can then be seen as part of the broad tradition of reaction against mass consumption, which is in part a tradition of reaction against the masses themselves. We have previously (Chapter 1) noted Carey's (1992) account of how a powerful strand of elitist contempt for the masses has permeated the British cultural establishment. And it is from that establishment, albeit in its somewhat denuded and diversified present form, that much of the anti-car rhetoric takes its cue. It is thus in the same tradition as the old elitist attacks on television, and on pop music. Anything which the people cleave to with such enthusiasm as they do their cars and their videos must be a bad thing. Greatest contempt is reserved for those vehicles which most clearly symbolise the car as democratic consumer good; hence the particular demonisation of Ford drivers.

You do not of course have to belong to the cultural elite to hold this sort of view; you can come to such opinions if, whoever you are, you are influenced by the metropolitan intelligentsia and their cultural output. Also we are all influenced by the ancient distinction between material progress and moral value (between 'civilisation' and 'culture'), and its assumption that the more material wealth and comfort there is in a society, the worse must be its moral condition. This distinction has always been an intellectual weapon of the elite, and is also at the service of technophobic polemic. In its contributions to modern convenience and freedom, the car has greatly offended those who would prefer that the means to go anywhere were not so widely distributed.

It is of course regrettable, and in many cases tragic, that parts of the countryside have been lost to roads, and there is no intention here to make any defence of the present British government's policies on transport. But much of the hostility to the car that is abroad among the enlightened middle classes is quite out of touch with the daily experience of the majority, and takes no account of the deep and positive changes which the car has facilitated in the lives of many. There need be no apology for summarising these benefits in the language of freedom and choice, since whatever claim may be laid on these terms by the far right they are central to environmentalist concerns. Environmentalism seems to provide us with the major contemporary example of the classical dilemma of the liberal polity, namely how to maximise freedom and choice in ways that are compatible with freedom and choice for others, and with the common good.

Psychoanalysis has nothing to contribute directly to the resolution of this dilemma. It can help us though to understand the feelings which become interwoven with arguments on both sides, from those wanting to defend or extend individual freedom – in this case, to use the car – and those seeking to curtail it. So let us now turn to look psychoanalytically at the hatred of the car, to complement the sociological location of it in traditions of elitism, and also to balance the psychoanalytic critique of the technophilic idealisation of the car.

For one thing, the car can symbolise or give expression to destructiveness. We know that it can be a murder weapon, an instrument for the easy devastation of lives. This places a heavy burden on the motorist, not only to drive carefully but also to live with the phantasies which being in control of such a potentially dangerous object are liable to activate. Psychoanalysis teaches us how readily phantasies of destruction can be triggered to influence experience and action, and it also highlights for us the psychic costs which the aggressive impulse can impose on us, even when we succeed in preventing ourselves from acting it out.

Many people believe from their everyday experience that this impulse is too frequently acted upon, especially by male drivers. If the arguments of this chapter have been correct, there is nothing in the intrinsic appeal of motor cars as rapid and elegant means of personal transport which should necessarily render them of significantly greater interest to men than women. But as much psychoanalytic work on gender has shown, in our present cultural arrangements there is too often an incitement to split between the genders, and for certain characteristics (especially more problematic ones) to be understood – and felt – to belong predominantly to men or to women. Thus it is clear that men are more implicated in aggressively technophilic and criminal uses of the car. But neither the seriousness of this as a social problem, nor the positive human significance of the car, should be allowed to obscure the other in an appraisal of its costs and benefits.

The car evokes powerful aggressive feelings, basically by virtue of what it does, though the arts of design and marketing have worked hard to intensify this effect. Yet it also requires of us that we restrain these feelings to a high degree in our actual use of the vehicle (though we may project them onto other drivers, or give expression to them in our opinions of other road users). There is more or less a taboo on physical contact between vehicles. Since the unconscious has difficulty in distinguishing between feelings acted on and those restrained, the evocation of aggressive phantasy – however careful and courteous the driver – will be accompanied by guilt. An image of the car therefore provides a psychic point around which can gather constellations of destructiveness and guilt. This applies not only to the individual motorist at the wheel but also in the patterns of feeling about the car in our culture at large, which enter into public discourse and which we all subscribe to and partake of whether or not we are drivers. The car will then, as a stimulant of destructiveness and guilt, have abundant meaning as a bad, persecuting object.

Now of course the car as an inert lump of technology can only stand for human feelings. We can use it to represent our feelings. But in the recent crystallisation of negative attitudes towards the car, what is happening to some extent is that the car is being seen as a concrete embodiment of these difficult feelings rather than a symbol of them, as a demonic agent in itself. In two 1992 television 'documentaries' the car has been presented as an alien, autonomous force to which humanity is enthralled, and as an evil drug to which we are addicted. And in a book called *Autogeddon*, a poem-cum-photoessay by Heathcote Williams, a fairly full-blown paranoid fantasy is elaborated, featuring the car as a 'mindless monster which threatens the planet itself'.

The notion of addiction is often used to describe our relation to a number of consumer goods. While it should be no more than a metaphor, and even then may still be misleading, it directs our attention to a second reason for the contemporary animosity towards the car. This is linked to a very obvious fact about it, which is that we are very dependent on the car. Many of those who rail against it nevertheless own one, and would find their lives seriously disrupted without it. The standard response that one would use public transport if it were better may to some extent be true, but for reasons of social geography as well as psychology there is no realistic scenario for a society like Britain in which the car does not continue to play a major role for the foreseeable future, however dramatic an improvement there might be in public services. And whatever the future may hold, the reality of the present is that we are dependent on the car. The object of dependency is at one level hated for its power over us, its power to let us down and frustrate us, and its power of control.

Individual cars, as fallible pieces of technology, are able to let us down, but the general sense of resentment towards the car for our dependence on it may also be related to the nature of our physical relationship with it. When we actually use it, we have to allow ourselves to be carried along by it, unable to get out of our seats and closely hedged in by steel and glass. Car sickness we may see as a response to this potentially claustrophobic environment, or perhaps as analogous to the panicky, nauseous response of a baby to being jogged and jerked around by a caretaker who is out of communication with it. Drivers, who are in control, do not as a rule get car sick. And even when we are not using the car, we are still controlled to some degree by its presence: the places we can walk in urban environments, and the sculpting of public space as a whole in the twentieth century, have been heavily determined by what is sometimes called, in a misleading reification, the 'needs of the car'.

The car may then take on qualities of the bad mother – a bad-environment mother, we might say if we were to play with Winnicott's term (see p. 62) – constricting, controlling, smothering. Especially in the context of our real-world dependence on it, this makes it likely that the car will be the object of some intense fears and apocalyptic scenarios. We could perhaps have predicted this anyway from the existence of technophilia: wherever there is idealisation, there must also be anxiety and hatred. The recent surges of anti-car feeling are the coming to the surface of our culture of technophobic feelings and imagery which were previously submerged by technophilic enthusiasms.

It is primarily social changes which have released this phobic underside, but at a psychodynamic level too technophilia will generate the expression of its opposite, as we recoil in fear from identifying with the image of technology as omnipotent. Some technologies are opposed out of the fear of 'playing God'. Here there is a kind of 'reaction-formation', as psychoanalytic language refers to an attempt to deal with some unacceptable feeling by trying to act in ways opposed to it. In this case, there is a conversion of the omnipotent technophilic impulse into its opposite – a rather desperate humility and a bitter aversion to the idea that human ingenuity might substantially alter the human condition. Extreme examples of this technophobic defence have been seen in relation to reproductive technologies. Reactionary uses of Christian belief have combined with some feminist viewpoints to decry the engineering of childbirth, on the grounds that a divine right is being transgressed, or an oppressive techno-patriarchal power extended.[3]

THE SOCIAL GRID

It has been argued that some of our relationships to the car, and by extension to many technologies, can be characterised as being in one of two modes, technophilic and technophobic. But this is not necessarily a counsel of despair, since technology is in reality not omnipotent nor univalent; it is no magical power for good or evil. It is part of human culture. So there is a third and optimal mode of relationship to it. In this mode, the unconscious resonances of the technology are felt and acknowledged, but contained within an experience which is shaped by the realistic limits as well as the powers of the technology, and also by its social nature.

There can be nothing intrinsically wrong with the ways in which we endow a technology such as the car with all kinds of meanings, since it is through similar unconscious mediations that we relate to everything in our material world, albeit not always so intensely or richly. So the optimal mode of relating to technology is not one in which we regard the technological objects simply as objects to be used for their functional purposes – getting from A to B, mixing food, permitting conversations with people thousands of miles away, or whatever. This is impossible. A car can never be just a means of getting from A to B, nor a telephone just a device for talking and listening through. The question is not whether there is a phantasy dimension to our relations with technologies, but what the content of those phantasies is, and what part they play in our overall use of the technologies and in our mental lives as a whole.

To clarify our thinking about this, we can return here to the general theory of culture which we can derive from psychoanalysis. Perhaps one of the most important contributions that psychoanalysis has to offer social understanding is in its insight that culture is not a higher human achievement pitted absolutely against brutal human nature. Culture is instead the process of constant struggle and interplay between primitive need and social constraint. Through this process we create subjectivities, institutions and material objects. The particular pleasures and satisfactions we gain from cultural participation are based on the integrations we can achieve between the contending forces. To use the language of classical psychoanalysis, this means achieving integrations between the pleasure and reality principles; it means sublimation. To put it in other terms, we must achieve fusions between sensuality and sociality; the body-ego must also be a social subject. And to put it in Kleinian terms, it means reparation, the predominance in the mind of loving feelings towards those primal objects (and their present-day representatives in the outside world) who have frustrated as well as nurtured the infantile self.

Technologies are material culture, and so are embedded in these tensions. Thus the optimal pleasures of car use consist not simply of the libidinal experience of speed and strength, nor simply in the regressive experience of being contained and protected. They consist of the combination of these meanings of the car with another set of meanings, with which all technologies are necessarily invested, in that they represent to us the society of which we are a part, the others with whom we must live, and the limits we must recognise if we are to enjoy relationships.

In the case of the car this means that pleasure comes not just from driving and controlling this libidinally polysemic object, but from doing so within a framework of rules and material boundaries, which are representative of society and our place in it: kerbs and other physical limits to navigable space, road markings, road signs, other vehicles and other people. It is these embodiments of the reality principle which, though they frustrate and deny the driver as libidinal subject, are themselves a source of powerful satisfactions since once we can negotiate them they constantly confirm our belonging in a containing and providing social matrix.

These pleasures are not there for the taking, of course; they have to be achieved through the learning of the necessary skills. Likewise the omnipotently-tinged pleasure we may derive from using our personal computers successfully depends on mastery of rules and procedures. Through these procedures which technologies enjoin upon us, sensuous experience and its hinterland of phantasy is mapped out within a social grid.

In Chapter 3 it was argued that sport was a major instance of this social framing of primitivity to create disciplines of delight. In Chapter 4 it was suggested that a similar psychodynamic configuration underlay attitudes in Britain towards the countryside. In automobile culture also we can find the same search for containment, both in the experience of the car body as a container and in the skilled use of that body within a containing social field. In the case of the car, the libidinality is perhaps more narcissistic, and the relationship to parental imagos more wishful and neurotic, than in the other examples explored in this book, but this need not be taken as a fixed state of affairs: cultures can change in their typical relationships to classes of objects.

To return, by way of concluding this chapter, to the politics of the environment: the major implication of what has been said is that environmentalism needs to develop a discourse which recognises the projective quality of our relationships with technology. It has already in various ways incorporated some understandings of technophilia (because these are obviously congenial to it); it needs to do the same for technophobia, and should not collude with technophobic sentiments. But since those sentiments press for environmentally desirable ends, in its concern with psychic truth psychoanalysis may be at odds with political expediency, even with political principle. This problem can potentially arise in any political application of psychoanalysis.

6   GOODS AND GOOD OBJECTS

PROSPECTS FOR A PSYCHOANALYSIS
OF CONSUMPTION

The home ground of psychoanalytic studies of everyday life is in the field of welfare and health services, in that psychoanalysis has developed primarily as a therapeutic discipline with broader applications which are usually seen as being within that field.[1] Nonetheless until fairly recently the influence of psychoanalytic ideas among health and welfare professionals has been very limited, due to various resistances amongst these workers to psychoanalytic thinking, and also to the general marginality of psychoanalysis in the wider culture.

Similarly in the political field: despite the growth in Britain in the last decade of a quite vigorous psychoanalytic culture, and of a small literature applying psychoanalysis to the political process, there is still very little space in public discourse for the kind of reflection that psychoanalysis can stimulate on such important current issues as nationalism, political leadership and urban riots. The nuclear war issue in the 1980s looked like fertile ground for the seeds of psychodynamic understanding, but beyond some rather loose notions about needs for enemies such understanding did not take root in the peace movement as a whole, let alone in the wider political culture.

To some extent the failure of psychoanalytic thinking to impress itself on a wider public may be due to shortcomings in the way in which it has been disseminated. Some ideal combination of the intellectual, the clinician and the plain-speaking citizen is the kind of person needed to bring analytic insights into more common discourse. There is also the justified suspicion of psychoanalytic approaches produced by the long tradition of reductive analytic theorising about the social world. But when psychoanalysis has something important and probably unique to say about, for example, the needs of children in foster care, or in families where sexual abuse is suspected, or about the inner life of the violent criminal, it is a tragedy if it is then so marginal, if not antithetical, to the ways of thinking prevalent among the professionals who work with such people and whose job it is to minimise emotional damage and contain destructiveness.

If we bring a psychoanalytic approach to the field of popular culture, we may at first notice no difference between this area and the fields of welfare and politics in terms of the general inhospitability of the intellectual climate to psycho-analysis, or at least to the kind of broadly Kleinian/object-relational psychoanalysis which is represented here. There are of course the Lacanian and related tendencies in cultural studies, but insofar as this has defined to that field what psychoanalysis is, and colonised the space so far allotted to it, this is a problem, since whatever their merits these ap-proaches do not exhaust the study of the unconscious in popular culture.

However if we turn to the fields of everyday consumption and advertising, we can no longer assume that people at large will usually tend to resist what psychoanalysis might have to say. It seems that common sense has a different quality to it in these domains. While references to unconscious anxieties and conflicts might be regarded as irrelevant in many discus-sions of professional practice, where obvious external pres-sures and problems may crowd in, there may be greater readiness to recognise their ubiquitous role in the selling and the use of motor cars, newspapers, chocolate, ice-cream and a host of other consumer goods. Perhaps it is easier for vulnerabilities to be acknowledged in the sphere of consump-tion than in that of work. Consumption is traditionally the more expressive domain, and therefore the one where idiosyn-crasy – and sexuality – have greater recognised licence.

It may be, even, that popular wisdom overestimates the actual effectivity of libidinal messages in the marketing of goods. Some recent work on advertising strikes a somewhat sceptical note on the question of the power of advertisements, at least in relation to their influence on purchasing decisions if not in their more general cultural impact.[2] While there is wide agreement on the importance of advertising as a topic for social research, the idea that it exerts a simple controlling influence now seems part of a dated, 1950s scenario in which fear of totalitarian forces was a dominant theme. Moreover, the popular equation of selling with sex is hardly commensurate with a psychoanalytic dissection of unconscious sexuality – the sex in question is usually an acutely felt dimension of everyday, conscious experience. So we must be cautious with the proposition that here in the domain of consumption there exists a receptive audience for the exploration of unconscious meanings.

Nevertheless, the influence of psychoanalytic thinking has been greater in this domain than elsewhere. Or perhaps we should say that there is a relatively high consonance of some psychoanalytic propositions with received ideas about why we consume the things we do. To put it this way does not assume that psychoanalysis itself is directly responsible for those ideas. It does suggest that there is at least a similarity, a convergence, between some of the concerns of psychoanalysis and some of the ideas we have about ourselves as consumers. Superficial though the popular understanding of sexuality may be by psychoanalytic standards, to see the consumer as to some extent a sexual creature does establish a place in the analysis of motivations for passion, irrationality and primitive bodily experience.

We can speculate on why there should be these differences in the influence of psychoanalytic ideas in different social spheres. We might reverse the oft-repeated notion that the problem with psychoanalysis is the difficulty of proving its efficacy, and suggest that in the world of mass consumption, where a large investment is continually made in evaluative research, psychoanalytic approaches are going to do well because they are effective – they can say something important about the qualities of ordinary experience and the determinants of everyday choice. In the welfare sector, in contrast, research into the effectiveness of different approaches is patchy, slow and cumbersome. It is also bedevilled by the lack of agreement on the criteria of success – nothing as consensual as a sales curve is to hand. It is thus possible for techniques and methods which are useless or counterproductive to flourish indefinitely, while the gains which can be made from others go largely unrecognised.

A second possibility is that psychoanalytic observations are more painful to make in some areas than others, and so are more resisted in some areas than others. The welfare services deal with loss, death, trauma, illness and damage. In this context of constant confrontation with bad experience and bad objects, the need for manic and schizoid defences is

great. Marketing and consumption are domains of goods and
the pleasures that can be obtained from them. Consumption
is at least on first impressions about drives rather than
defences; it is a libidinally positive domain, where satisfaction
and fulfilment in some form are usually the aim, while care
must focus on destructive forces and on the work of renunciation. (We shall be qualifying this simple distinction later on,
but there is a truth in it.) While it may be no more than
embarrassing to recognise the sexual or narcissistic elements
in one's choice of consumer goods, it may be psychically
much more threatening to dwell on the aggressive or omnipotent impulses at play in one's experience of illness or in
intrafamilial conflict. The unthinkable hovers in the doctor's
surgery and around the social work case conference in a way
that it does not in the department store or leisure centre. Of
course defences abound in our experience of ourselves as
consumers, but they may be less massive and less inimical to
psychoanalytic reflection.

MARKET RESEARCH MEETS THE UNCONSCIOUS

There are some footholds for beginning such reflection in the
use of psychoanalytic ideas in market research. Psychoanalytic
thinking and practice has developed in professional and
political cultures which are on the whole at a considerable
distance from the worlds of commercial research and marketing. Nonetheless we can trace historically a major influence
that the psychoanalytic tradition has had upon the development of consumer and market research.

The key chapter in this story concerns the development of
what came to be known as 'motivational research'. One of the
main originators of this approach, Ernest Dichter, was an
Austrian psychologist who took his Viennese training to the
United States in the late 1930s and began there to apply it to
market research. He was not analytically trained, but inter-war
psychology, especially in Europe, was much more hospitable to
psychoanalytic approaches than it subsequently became. Influenced by cultural anthropology as well as by the methods of
dynamic clinical work, Dichter (1960; 1964) brought a new
depth to commercial research, focusing on the social and
biographical contexts of specific acts of consumption, and
tuning in to the sensual qualities of objects (e.g. the shape of a

bar of soap in the palm of the hand) and to the phantasy-meanings of different materials (e.g. the different pleasures to be had from wood and from glass). He advocated holistic, qualitative methods to unravel the complex dynamics of motivation. He introduced the idea that objects and brands have 'personalities', and was well aware that they do so because people project themselves into products. As he put it, 'Objects have a soul' (1960, p.86), placed in them by cultural traditions and individual needs, and the interplay between them.

So, when Dichter received a commission from a food company to study the market position of soup, he proposed 'to understand the real meaning of soup' (1960, p. 147). 'The real meaning of soup': the cynic might smile at this, thinking that the essential triviality of market research was here revealed. The anthropologist would have no such reaction, and would be alert for what the results of the market research might say about the society in which the soup is consumed. Dichter's research team would talk to people about soup at some length: what kinds they consumed, when, where, with whom, why, what they liked and felt about it. They would do desk research on the history of soup, and on cultural differences in soup consumption, and search for significant literary or cinematic appearances of soup. Market researchers today would not need to do so much of this background work from scratch, although the confidentiality of much commercial research is a major problem in the collation of existing knowledge.

Dichter's work initiated the rise, after the Second World War, of MR – motivational research – to a position of some prominence in the market research industry, which hitherto – since its emergence in the US in the 1910s (Lazer, 1973) – had been more concerned with statistical and descriptive work than with depth-psychological analysis.

The pre-eminence of motivational research in the commercial field did not last all that long, being overshadowed in the 1960s and 1970s by new computer-based quantitative approaches. It had a lasting impact, however, in that concepts of unconscious desire became part of the general vernacular of commercial research, and projective testing became widely recognised as a standard technique.

We should note here a distinction between two kinds of market research. There are on the one hand studies of how goods and services are experienced, and on the other those of how advertisements, marketing campaigns, corporate images and the like are experienced. In the former type it is the substantive use of the goods that is examined; consumers' reactions to or views about actual goods or services are being investigated, and there is at least the possibility for the results of the research to be fed into the process of product development in such a way as to lead to products which more closely fit the expressed needs and wishes of a majority. This is a kind of 'democratising' conception of market research, which sees it as converging with one strand of the consumerist movement. In studies of advertising and the like, however, it is the impact of imagery upon the consumer's buying behaviour that is of principal interest, and the aim of the research may be no more noble than finding out how to sell more of a particular product or product range. Once again, though, people's tastes are being mapped, and attention may be given to the quality of the relationships between companies and consumers, and to the quality of the social presence of the corporation.

From the viewpoint of psychosocial research the distinction may be unimportant; it may be at least as interesting to know what people make of an advert as it is to know what kind of goods they want. Certainly as far as psychoanalytic research is concerned, it is all in the realm of symbol and meaning, with which actual products are saturated as much as are advertising images. In practice, the relatively small amount of work that is now conducted using an explicitly psychoanalytic framework is probably more concerned with pure imagery rather than with product development or service delivery. Thus for example an Italian research company has developed a method for evaluating the impact of advertising jingles based on the work of the analyst Franco Fornari and his particular conceptualisation of the impact of unconscious phantasy on everyday experience. They use jingles as the stimulus material for a series of associative and projective tests, and aim to identify how even a few bars of mundane music can activate what Fornari termed the 'primary ideas of life' – images of birth, death, kinship and sexuality – and evoke in the listener hidden scenarios of affect and relationship (Frontori et al, 1989).

Why MR and the other examples of psychoanalytically influenced market research are important outside of the commercial sphere is because they suggest some directions in which a psychoanalytically informed analysis of consump-

tion ought to look in order better to understand why we
consume in the ways that we do. And in exploring consumption, we are exploring culture in general.

A key contribution of psychoanalysis to the theory of
culture, from Freud onwards, has been in its statements of
the idea that cultural institutions, if they are to thrive, must
combine authority and restraint with the opportunity for
those participating in them to meet some of their primitive
needs – that is, they must require adherence to the reality
principle while also compensating us for subordinating ourselves to it. This should apply to the institutions and
practices of consumer culture as much as it does to
religion, which was the example from which Freud originally
derived this idea. A number of themes are put into focus
both by this psychoanalytic theorisation of consumption, and
by the empirical findings of MR and related approaches.
(Of course a problem here is that most commercial research
is not published, but from that which is available it is
possible to make some generalisations.)

Firstly, a psychoanalytically guided exploration of the
field of consumption yields the conclusion that consumer
goods and the imagery asociated with them can be understood as a projective system, to use a term favoured by the
psychoanalytic anthropologists. Our experiences of things
and images is derived in part from our projections onto
them, from the shaping effects that our internal worlds can
have on our perceptions of the external world. This means
that we are not, in our apparent enthralment to certain
kinds of goods and in our constant exposure to advertising,
entirely the victims of manipulation, of imposed values and
deceitful promises. Rather we confront ourselves, albeit as
constructed through the mediations of marketers, advertisers
and other professionals of the symbolic. We cannot hold
others entirely responsible for our own projections.

These projections operate at two levels, or in two phases.
When you look at an advertisement, or savour the taste of a
new kind of crisp, or contemplate the lines of a car, you are
of course projecting elements of your inner world into the
experience. But the stimulus material for that experience –
the advertising images and words, the recipe for the crisps,
the design of the car – is likely itself to have been selected
from a range of possibles according to the projections put
onto it by other people – the subjects of market research.

This is because most advertisements and new products are tested in research before their release. The data gathered by market researchers on people's responses to a range of possible images or products may have played a considerable part in determining what is presented to the rest of us. This will not always be the case, and there is a school of thought among designers and the 'creative' people in advertising which sees market research as likely to stifle creativity if its results determine the final product. It is feared that such research can only represent the dreary conventionality of the public, or even the 'lowest common denominator'.

Yet however one evaluates its impact, there is little doubt that market research substantially shapes many of the goods and images which surround us. The hope of the market strategist is, to put it psychoanalytically, that the market research will have predicted the range of projections which people are likely to make onto the final product, and will give some assurance that these will be of an optimal kind, that is, that people will not find an advertisement to be pretentious, or a crisp to taste unhealthy, or a car to look ungainly. The meanings which we find in adverts and goods are at least in part our individual creations, though they are likely to be within an affective range defined by those of us who are the subjects in market research exercises.

CONSUMPTION, REGRESSION AND GOOD OBJECTS

To focus on this projective quality of consuming is to take a very different tack from the semiological and discourse analysis approaches which have tended to predominate in cultural studies. These see the meanings of goods as deriving from the whole network of meanings in which they are embedded. 'Soup' is a sign or cluster of signs which have meaning only in relation to other signs – the whole grammar of food, the language of nurture, and so on. In this way of thinking, rather than subjects creating meanings, meanings create subjects.

In the British psychoanalytic tradition, however, an irreducibly humanist axiom states that individual subjects with basic symbolic vocabularies rooted in the bodily experience of early care are sites for the generation of meaning, which is then fed into the circulation of signs. Perhaps, though, through dialogue with discourse analysis and related approaches this axiom might be tempered and elaborated in productive ways.

Discourse analysis notwithstanding, the understanding of consumption as being fundamentally about meanings endowed by the consumers is basic to most social theorising about it, from Thorstein Veblen (1899) and his notion of 'conspicuous consumption' onwards. It is widely agreed that as consumers we express ourselves through the meanings with which the objects and activities of consumption are endowed. In his recent major contribution to the theory of consumption, the sociologist Colin Campbell (1987) has expanded on this theme by linking the expressive impulse of consumerism to the Romantic movement and to what he calls the 'imaginative' type of hedonism which is the main cultural legacy of Romanticism. The pleasures of consumption, he argues, are basically imaginative – we imagine what a new commodity will bring us, and the inevitable failure of the reality completely to live up to the anticipation is what drives us on to the next purchase, with hope eternal.

Translating this kind of theory into psychoanalytic language, we could say that the consumer is searching for an external embodiment of an idealised object, which being ideal is unattainable. Alternatively, we can take up a suggestion by Robert Young (1989), which is that many consumer goods function as transitional objects, that is as bridges between self and otherness. They provide for the consumer experiences of sensual enfolding, in which the boundary between self and object is regressively but helpfully blurred. Immersion in stereo sound, the all-over caress of bath oil, and the deep comfort of a dressing gown, are some of his examples.

These are both very illuminating perspectives on many examples or aspects of consumption. However the emphasis here is on consumption as involving a different kind of object search, something less regressive than a quest for either ideal or transitional objects. Later in this chapter we will explore the idea that we try to create in the world of external goods a universe of good rather than ideal objects, that is to say objects which – like cultural institutions – both gratify and also limit and contain us, which represent to us both satisfaction and reality. In our consumption of goods we are then trying to introject them as good objects or to enact some kind of good object relationship with them.

One feature of good objects (especially in the particular, perhaps somewhat expanded sense in which I am using the term here) is that they are stable and constant. What then of the consumer's endless desire for the new? We cannot plausibly ascribe our constant thirst for new goods entirely to the blandishments of advertising and to the constant drive to expand markets. It seems likely that our spontaneous desires for greater comfort and convenience would result in a steady stream of new goods and services, even under conditions of much less intensely profit-driven, obsolescence-creating economic activity than we are used to. There is then an ineradicable tension between on the one hand the desire for the new, and on the other, the need for stability and sameness.

According to one broad tradition of psychoanalytically oriented cultural criticism, the unrelenting stimulation of the consumer's appetite by new commodities has a destructive effect on the modern psyche. By requiring us continually to move on to something new, it contributes to a condition of schizoid or narcissistic withholding from deep, stable relationships. Capacities for forming stable attachments to people, already damaged at root by the impact of market relations and other aspects of modern society upon parenting capacities, are thus further eroded, and an exploitative or at least irresponsible attitude towards the material world is encouraged.

However the lust for the new cannot be blamed entirely on the manipulations of marketing. Connoisseurs of the motor car especially will be very familiar with the unique appeal of the object in its *new* form, and with an immediate, often sensuous quality to this appeal which is hard to attribute to marketing alone.

THE BLISS OF THE NEW

There are two forms which newness can take in commodities: one is that of the new model, that of the startling new design or stylistic innovation – the appearance in everyday life of a new sign which commands attention and evokes desire. This is part of the phenomenon of fashion, that is of the hunger for new signs, the compulsion to recirculate signs, to revise meanings and to recombine images, which is often taken to be central to the dynamic of modern consumerism (see Campbell, 1987; Wilson, 1985). It is also part of the process of technological change, by which new goods may make functional advances over older ones. In both these respects – semiotic and practical – marketing may be necessary to help us generate the new meanings, or to appreciate the functional improvements, but it does not create in us the needs for new significations, or for greater convenience.

The second form of the new is more mundane, and even harder to see as a false construction; it is that of the fresh, unused and pristine object – the shoes on the shop rack, the car in the showroom or on the road in its first few weeks of 'life', the spotless refrigerator interior. The delight here is in the sheer perfection of the good, in its unsullied surface and powers not weakened by use. In the case of some re-usable objects which are not literally consumed, the new may be – in functional terms – no better than the old, and may be worse than it. The shoes have to be worn in, the new model of car may be riddled with design and manufacturing faults, and so on, or may at least take some getting used to. The new can be cold and alien. Another of the dynamics of consumerism is based upon the tension and interplay between our needs to individualise and become attached to our possessions, and, on the other hand, the delight in the unpossessed new, the temptation to replace objects with functionally similar but new ones.

This temptation is not always a matter of fashion. The second kind of neophilia (to adapt Christopher Booker's [1969] term) is a simple pleasure in the new commodity, whether or not it is fashionable, and whether or not it is operationally 'better'.

It is not difficult to suggest what might be the psychic roots of this pleasure. The delight in the new is a narcissistic phenomenon. An experience of the self as ideal can be recovered or confirmed through possession or use of the new object. As we contemplate or imagine the pristine, new good we project onto it our images of wholeness and purity; we can safely lodge them in the blemish-free surface of the purchase, and then re-introject them in the process of purchase, ownership and use. These narcissistic projections are not very powerful; though the first scuff or scrape to appear may be particularly distressing, our relationship to new goods is usually no more than a minor, low-key enactment of a psychic scenario.

But the scenario is a central one in mental and economic life, and we may hold it partly responsible for some of the enormous waste perpetrated by the affluent societies. The huge consumption of paper and plastic in order to create entirely new place settings for the most fleeting customers in cafés and restaurants, or to produce impressive packagings for trivial purchases, could not do its work of wooing the consumer if we did not have this need for the immaculate. This is one way in which a sentiment traditionally understood as religious has been displaced onto the material world, although to speak of 'displacement' implies that its *original* nature is religious rather than free-floating primitive narcissism. In any case, unless we want to recreate some theological space for this pristine self, we need to be thinking of how it can find greater variety of less wasteful expressions in material culture.

The best place for an idealised object is, so to speak, in the shadow of the integrated object, or lodged within it, so that the best efforts of the individual to restore the ideal are directed at the real world rather than against or wishfully outside of it. There could be considerable scope for projects to discipline the desire for the immaculate in the service of environmentalist goals – repairing, protecting, cleaning-up, and so on – if such projects could stress their continuity with savouring the bliss of the new, rather than taking the high moral ground and opposing themselves to such pleasure, which leaves them at risk of being seen as regressive or hair-shirt sentimentality. Some practices which are currently hobbies or 'alternatives' around the margins of consumer culture may have value as examples or forerunners of new modes of consumption which could accommodate in conservationist ways our tendencies to make narcissistic projections into goods. The 'restoration' of 'classic' cars, for example (which now includes the mass-production models of fifteen to twenty years ago), offers a very different take on the consumer's experience from the idea of the 'second-hand', with its cruel blow to the narcissistic wish to be the one and only.

CONTINUITIES IN THE STREAM OF GOODS

The suspicion of the new and of rapid obsolescence found in the critical psychoanalysis of culture (actually, of course, a traditional critique onto which psychoanalytic ideas have been grafted) gives us nonetheless an important moral purchase on many aspects of everyday life. However there are some additional considerations which should be mentioned. One is that the capitalist market itself provides for some kind of stability and sameness in the objects consumed through the phenomenon of branding.

The competition between brands, and the seductive assault on the consumer by brand images, are often thought of as being at the cold heart of capitalist consumerism, as a driving force behind the empty promises and profligate waste of the consumer society. We can admit the force of these moral and pragmatic critiques while also making some space for the view that branding may have other effects. It is a commonplace among market researchers that people buy the same brand because they want the same as they had before; they know what they are getting. Risk and uncertainty are eliminated, and the corrosive effect of constant novelty is held off.

Branding contains the anxiety about consuming more and different objects not only through the consumption of images of the brand as eternal and constant, but also through our experience of the actual good itself. One pair of Levi's is much like any other, Coke and Pepsi taste the same wherever they are bought, and – in the furthest development of this principle – the whole experience of going to McDonald's, from the greetings of the staff to the taste of the burger, is remarkably similar the world over. The fast-food industry is clearly based on a number of other psychological principles, such as the attractions of more or less instant warm nourishment (feeding on demand), and of food that can be eaten with the fingers. But predictable sameness is one key component of its success (see George Ritzer's interesting Weberian analysis of fast-food rationalisation, 1992).

The even constancy of fish fingers and baked beans is widely understood to be one of the reasons why so many children cleave to them. This is usually more a matter of homogenous texture and predictable taste rather than of brand specificity, but it points to one likely psychological

basis of brand loyalty. The sameness of branded goods fits in
with the phantasy of an endlessly plentiful maternal object
who is never weakened nor changed by our demands upon
her, and who would never expose us to unwelcome surprise.
Paranoid fears of being poisoned by a bad, vengeful mother
are the most primitive psychic layer of the anxiety about
surprise in the context of children's food. Adults, it might be
argued, should be less under the sway of such anxiety, and
should therefore be less needing of sameness in their daily
consumption. Nevertheless, in a society of abundance it is a
reasonable demand that a good experience should be repro-
ducible in its aesthetic specifics, regressive though this may in
part be, and branding is a means of achieving this.

It is not only specifically *maternal* imagery which resonates
around the brand. Wernick (1991) has suggested that corporate identities can mobilise phantasies of providing parents,
such that a major corporation may be felt to be the 'parent' of
its subsidiary companies or its brands, as well as of the
consumers of its goods. Blood lines and familial resemblances
may then be felt to run through the world of goods (as can
be seen very clearly in automobile design), and in brand
allegiance we may be affirming a sense of kinship, or assert-
ing a tie to a powerful and generous patriarch.

Branding aside, there is a further way of understanding the
impact of endless novelty upon the psyche which does not
prematurely resign itself to the triumph of new goods over old
internal objects. Instead we can focus upon the continuing
tension between the two, and suggest that far from being
submerged beneath the rising tide of commerce, our inner
store of good object relationships is more likely to be
generating ways of absorbing the challenge of the new and
the unfamiliar. We therefore find ourselves engaged in a
search for ways of thinking and talking about our goods and
our choices among them which mitigate for us the tensions
between the familiar and the better. Perhaps the most typical
way of doing this is by constructing an identity for the new
which links it to the old.

Advertising obviously plays a role here, in for example
some of the campaigns based on nostalgic themes. Campaigns
for Hovis bread and Heinz soup are two recent British
examples that come to mind, though neither of these products
realistically needs dressing up in the garments of tradition and
stability, since they have been around for longer than most of

us. These are cases of the actual longevity of a product being exploited, rather than of an image of continuity being constructed. Better examples of the latter would be those campaigns which stress the 'classic' qualities of a new product, whether car or hair conditioner, and so seek to reassure the consumers that far from being engaged in a destructive pursuit of the new and better they are contributing to a project of restoring or preserving the old and better.

THE GUILTY CONSUMER

The anxiety about consuming the new overlaps with, and leads us on to consider, another tension, which is perhaps the most fundamental to consumption, and about which psychoanalysis, as a specific body of knowledge, can speak most distinctively. This is the tension between desire and guilt. In the last twenty years, concerns about the environment have added new dimensions, both realistic and in phantasy, to the long tradition of guilt in the mind of the consumer. This guilt has a number of sources. Dichter focused particularly on affluence as a source of guilt, the 'burden of the good life', as he called it. It seems that a sizeable proportion of his work was concerned with finding ways of presenting goods that minimised the guilt which people felt at consuming them.

Guilt does not of course attach itself only to the consumption of goods which might be widely regarded as gratuitous luxuries or which are known to involve some wanton destruction in their making. It also attaches itself, at least unconsciously, to the consumption of what widely might be regarded as innocent necessities, as a consequence of phantasy scenarios in which others are damaged through not having these goods, or have been damaged through the subject acquiring them.

Sometimes the phantasy hangs on a large hook in reality. One puts a bowl of breakfast cereal down on a newspaper, noting that it covers a photograph of a dying child and a famine relief appeal. Munching on, one ruminates on what previous generations of one's family, whose lives are imagined to have been narrow and hard, might have had for breakfast. Typically we do not dwell on these thoughts, and they are soon forgotten as the day gathers pace, but they presumably gather together and shadow every meal.

Since the heyday of motivational research, however, this level of experience has not been much examined in market research – indeed, it has probably never been fully explored. This is after all the dark side of consumption. We are talking here about fears that a loved object has been irretrievably spoiled, or a sibling cruelly deprived, or – more primitively, when depressive anxiety slips back into persecutory terror – about fears of being castrated, poisoned, devoured, deserted or some other terrible fate as a punitive consequence of what to the onlooker may seem to have been an innocuous, everyday act of consumption, but which in phantasy was an expression of boundless greed.

This is, among other things, the unconscious, irrational level of environmentalism, about which Janine Chasseguet-Smirgel has written (1986), although she was referring specifically to the German Greens and was linking the guilt to a *real* historical event – the Holocaust – rather than to psychic universals. It is also a factor to be taken into account in understanding the prevalence in recent years of 'food scares', in some of which there has apparently been a regression to paranoid fears of retaliation from a much-abused Mother Nature.

We are piling together here anxieties which relate to different developmental levels, and which are treated in different ways by different theories. We need not apologise for this as their empirical occurrence may be in such a tangled heap, which we can best refer to under the general rubric of guilt, of a more or less primitive kind.

Again, as with the tension between the new and the familiar, advertising appears to play a role in soothing the distressed consumer, since many advertisements deal explicitly with the problem of guilt. Sometimes they do this simply by inciting a libidinal revolt – the 'Go on, spoil yourself!' line – but more often it is by engaging with the guilt, seeking to melt away its intransigence or to harmonise it with the consuming impulse (analogous to the way in which an obsessional symptom links the savage superego with prurience in a punitive preoccupation with dirt or danger). Take for example a Volkswagen advertisement which says 'We put people in front of cars', and shows a baby in a pushchair placed alarmingly in front of the nose of a VW. All the murderousness which drivers may sometimes feel, or more often fear in themselves, and particularly also the allegedly anti-nurturant attitude which we are now told characterises the car driver, all this is drawn strikingly to our conscious attention by the visual image. But the words reassure us; we know that the visual is only a play on the words, which tell us that our anxieties about our destructiveness are not appropriate here. The ad has then lured our guilt into the open, in order to contain it.

The difference between an obsessional symptom and an advertisement is that the former is distressing while the latter, usually, is not. (Some people find some ads distressing, but this is at least ostensibly on the grounds of public morality rather than because they evoke an inner conflict.) This ad may or may not have helped to persuade more people to buy Volkswagens; of more general significance is its potential impact on all motorists. It may make some non-VW drivers feel better – surely they too can put people before cars. Or, if the image was not well-chosen, it may make them feel worse about driving.

Further, there is the possibility of the advertisement (which was the subject of an extensive poster and press campaign in 1991) having an impact even upon those not in the market for cars who may give it only a casual glance. One of the characteristics of advertisements that renders them so significant in the study of culture is their unavoidable presence in public space. Whatever particular goods they may be promoting, they set an agenda for our everyday experience in their use (usually through skilfully constructed, rich and powerful imagery) of psychosocial themes. They do not create these themes: insecurity of various kinds, envy and guilt are not foisted upon an innocent public by manipulative copywriters. But they do articulate these themes in specific ways that help to shape the predominant experience of self and society, and of course to link the resolution of problems to the consumption of goods.

The recent controversial Benetton campaigns – much attended to by cultural commentators! – may also be relevant here. These poster and print ads have consisted simply of striking images of suffering and conflict, for example, the bloody uniform of a dead Bosnian soldier. Benetton argued they were breaking out of a 'commercial fairyland which pretends war doesn't exist ... trying to get important issues debated ... if it gets people talking about the issue that is good' (Marina Galanti for the company, quoted in Culf, 1994).

Such ads arguably do subvert the tendency for the discourse of consumption to be used in familiar escapist ways, and they point towards some politically interesting possibilities for changes in the relationships between the different spheres of life, as part of the overall trend towards greater permeability between work, leisure and social responsibilities. At the same time, however, they may, by creating an acknowledged space for guilt and social concern in the process of consumption, ease the mind of the consumer about consuming.[3] This is probably not part of Benetton's deliberate strategy, and the effect may not be to make more purchases in Benetton shops more likely, but again the point for social analysis is not so much the commercial effects of the ads as the wider consequences of their social presence.

What this discussion is edging towards here is a view of advertising as discharging – among its many social roles – a psychologically helpful function, helpful that is from the viewpoint of the consumer who wants to be able to consume at minimum psychological cost. No doubt this kind of positive analysis of the social role of advertising has been hit upon before by apologists for that industry, but that is no reason for those of us who do not have a brief to defend advertising to reject it out of hand. We are simply seeing here an example of the characteristic tendency of psychoanalytic thinking when applied to social phenomena, which is to undermine conceptions of the social world as a place in which some people (usually conceived of as a dominant minority) do things to the rest of us, who are conceived of as innocent – or at worst as passive – in this process.

SMOKING AND REALITY

So much here for our relationship to images, though there is of course much more to be said about that. To conclude, we will return to our relationship to actual goods. The general thesis has been that in our relationship to goods we seek not just satisfactions but also confirmation of the restraints upon us and of our ties to others – confirmation, in short, of our social being, which consists of these restraints and ties. As a final example we will take one of the icons of addictive consumerism, albeit one now perhaps passing into recent history, the cigarette.

The cigarette is obviously about libidinal satisfaction, about oral need, but is also about the formation and maintenance of social bonds. How many friendships and families have begun with cigarettes, how many social interchanges have been mediated and regulated by the exchange of cigarettes? There is sociality aplenty here, as well as brute sucking. Sometimes the social value of a cigarette might contradict and outweigh its sensual value: you really didn't feel like another one, but you had one because somebody you wanted to get to know was offering you one.

Further, the cigarette has also carried some meaning of authority and maturity, sometimes in a world-weary, urban sort of way (the Bogart cigarette), sometimes in a spirit of more open-air mastery (the Marlboro cigarette). Now these meanings of tough maturity were obviously given to the cigarette by cultural and sub-cultural discourses in which it figured (by what might be described as its discursive location behind the school bike sheds). We can confirm this cultural determination of meanings by citing the shifts which have taken place in them (see Schudson, 1986). In the early days of cigarettes, in the late nineteenth century, they were regarded in the United States as a feminine way of consuming tobacco, and were for that reason banned from the US Navy. Later, after its take-up by men (largely through the impact of World War One on various social habits), the cigarette in the US and Europe became an important emblem of female emancipation, as it more recently has been in some Muslim countries. Since our experience of the reality principle is heavily inflected by gender, we must assume that these variations in the gender meanings of the cigarette will qualify its unconscious significance.

Yet at another level the meaning of the cigarette as *maturity* has been derived from the material experience of the object itself, which may explain why the cigarette was selected for the role of signifier of maturity. The cigarette is about sucking, but what you get when you suck is not warm, smooth milk, not nourishment, but an abrasive, dry smoke. Smoking is about disappointment, or rather about the overcoming of disappointment. The smoker again and again experiences the hollowness and toxicity of the smoke, and has the repeated experience of bringing that under control. One of the core pleasures of smoking concerns the experience of controlling this unpleasant smoke as it hits

the back of the mouth, by taking it right inside oneself and
then expelling it with imperious nonchalance. There is
probably a bad object being controlled here, by introjection
(actually by literal incorporation), and it might be argued
that the addiction to smoking is a compulsive attachment to
an alluring bad object.

But the cigarette is a good object in the sense that it
brings not only gratification and social engagement, but also
this experience of manageable disenchantment and symbolic
maturation. It also absorbs back some of the badness; in
smoking, the pristine and tantalising cigarette is turned into
an odious stub which can then be disposed of. As such, it is a
kind of containing object, containing the expelled badness of
the smoker.

This is all apart from the pharmacological properties of
nicotine, which helped to select tobacco rather than some
other plant as the content of the cigarette. These of course
are the writer's associations to smoking; they could probably
be tested if we had access to the reports that Dichter's
Institute for Motivational Research would have written for
American tobacco companies in the 1940s and 1950s. They
are offered here not as a confirmed analysis but to illustrate
the kind of primary generation of meaning which can take
place in the consumer's relation to goods, and the quite
complex pattern of object-relationships which can develop
within the contradictions between regressive desire and
mature renunciation.

The cigarette has of course been discursively shifted over
the last two decades so that it is now widely experienced as
a bad object; the kind of harsh, industrial disenchantment
which it symbolises has been culturally discredited in the
era of service industries, child-centredness and the growth
movement, while social changes have meant that it creates
enmity more often than friendship. The growth of knowledge
about 'passive smoking' and its effects has brought to our
attention another reality. While the threat of damage to
one's own health could be subordinated to the quest for
toughness and disenchantment, the threat of damage to
others' health is not so easily shrugged off or defiantly
ignored.

The automobile has also for some people recently under-
gone a similar relocation across the divide between good
and bad objects, as was seen in Chapter 5. So the

individual consumer's relation to goods is clearly part of wider historical trends, at the same time as being determined by the creative work which our projections constantly do upon the objects of our experience. Consumption (like other cultural practices) involves the projection of object representations which are linked with sensual gratification but also confirm us in our social being and in the reality principle.

7   MUSIC FOR ALL THE FAMILY

A PERSPECTIVE ON POP MUSIC

Whatever the subjects of the preceding chapters had been, there would have been easy connections to make with that of this one.[1] Pop music is now one of the most ubiquitous and evident commodities in popular culture, an accompaniment to other forms of cultural experience and stimulant to consumption. As a cultural form of great sensuousness and adaptability, pop music is a register for many of today's dominant tensions and conflicts around identity, community and gender, and of their unconscious concomitants in patterns of need and phantasy.

Pop music is often thought of as marking the break between the young generation and its parents. There are good reasons for seeing it in this way. New waves and trends in pop may seem designed to be incongenial or incomprehensible to older people, whose cultural experience was formed in an earlier period. Adolescents' immersion in sub-cultures based on specific forms of music is sometimes the focal point of conflict with their parents. Images of youthful rebellion and intergenerational distance are traditionally associated with popular music.

Also, pop helps to organise the young person's development as a consumer, appearing as it does both as cultural product and as advertising and shopping soundtrack in all areas of consumption, where personal identity is sought and affirmed. In these evident ways, then, pop music is about separation, the psychological process by which we become established as individuals. It is a cultural institution which has as a major function the provision of symbolic materials for us to use in working through or containing anxieties about separation. As such it has a positive psychocultural meaning, although not all kinds of pop music may partake of this, and there are some arguments to be had about which types of music and which musicians may be seen to embody it most or least.

We will eschew any attempt here to divide up the field in this way, and settle instead for some positively illustrative case studies, which will hopefully elaborate this conception of pop in a way consistent with the general contention that cultural institutions are most successful when they combine the highest possible levels of both pleasure and reality, when they can acknowledge the regressive or bodily impulses but contain them within a framework of social, rule-bound otherness.

The separation at issue in pop can be understood on two levels. One is the social and historical, of which a little more will be said in the next chapter. The other is the personal and individual: pop clearly plays a role in the separation struggles of many adolescents. In part we can understand the process of separation in terms of sexuality. In the emotional struggles of adolescence, sexuality is a central force, and is the one least amenable to integration into the individual's relationships with their parents. Indeed, unlike the equally powerful forces of aggression and dependency needs, it cannot find direct expression within the family. To the considerable extent that the appreciation of pop music requires involvement in a sexualised sub-culture outside the family, then it may contribute substantially to emotional development. It provides a range of social relationships and a language of dress, demeanour and so on through which emergent sexuality can speak – not to mention the language of 'love' which predominates in song lyrics.

But although pop is often celebratory of romantic love, in the manner typical of some leading popular genres of film and fiction, its characteristic mood is melancholic, and its predominant concerns are with *lost* love. Viewed psychoanalytically, this passion is double-edged. It is part of the adolescent transition, and its later echoes, away from the family of origin and towards engagement in the vicissitudes of adult relationships and toleration of their pain. Yet it is also regressive; behind the lost love sung about there is the earlier loss of the enveloping love of the parents for the baby and young child, grown out of but still yearned for, and remaining a potent force in the mind.

The separation complex therefore compounds movement away from the parents with a reliving of early relationships; rejecting and self-assertive feelings are mixed with regressive ones. Among psychological theories, psychoanalysis has a particularly strong purchase on the depth of the regressive impulses. It is also distinctive in its stress on the particular role of sexuality; though most psychological theories agree on the importance of the separation struggle in adolescence, not all would agree on the nature and centrality of sexuality as psychoanalysis defines it, nor on the suggestion that the erotic dramas into which the adolescent enters are at one level replays of earlier relationships and conflicts within the family.

Anxieties about separation, about the body and its functions, and about the reliability of others, and problems in the management of hostile and ambivalent feelings, are the stuff of infancy and childhood, of relationships between children and their parents. In adolescence these issues are re-encountered at a different level, where they can become fully sexualised and where permanent separation from parents is on the agenda. Many other people, sexual partners and friends especially, now play important roles in the drama in their own right, but one subtext remains focused on the parents. On a psychoanalytic view, deeply buried feelings about early caregivers are the ground of being, and provide a framework within which all subsequent experience is lived.

Psychoanalysis always draws our attention to this familial grounding of all experience, even when that experience is concerned with growing out of and away from one's family of origin. The paradox is only an apparent one; in order to separate, or to 'individuate' as some psychologists refer to the process by which a psychologically viable person develops, many feelings about the persons from whom one is separating have to be worked through.

With this in mind we can consider pop music as an area of cultural production and experience in which young people (and increasingly not-so-young people) are replaying, and perhaps working through, aspects of their relationships with their parents. We can discover beneath its apparently non-familial discourse some deep structures of filial sentiment. In pop as elsewhere images of idealised, hated and loved parents can be found, and the uses made of these images determines the moral content of the music. Its producers and consumers are in conversation with their internal images of their parents, even though they might be out of communication with their external ones.

There is some evidence for this in the way that the music and its associated styles are themselves in conversation with earlier pop trends. The pastiche and nostalgia frequently found (in popular culture as a whole, not just music) suggest an attempt to inhabit the experience of earlier generations. They illustrate the child's strategy of hoping to acquire by an outward imitative process something of the inner substance of the parent. We have now seen several such appropriations of the music of the hippy period, and at the time of writing there is a certain vogue for the early to mid-1970s music of Abba *et al*; perhaps when the children of the punk generation become a little older and become cultural producers themselves we shall hear affectionate re-recordings of the New Wave classics from the late 1970s.

Perhaps the basic way in which pop music carries on the conversation with parents is through words, and the feelings linked to them. We should give some thought here to the language in which pop, more than any other medium, speaks to us about relationships, particularly in the use of the word 'baby'. As a term of endearment betwen adults, 'baby' indicates the persistence in adult sexual relationships of some of the feelings (of possession, dependence and desire) which originate in early experiences of being looked after. Significantly, 'Daddy' is another term for a sexual partner.[2] Interestingly, 'Mummy' is not, though a sexualised 'Mama' can be found in blues lyrics. While ostensibly dealing in a language of adult sexual love, pop works also in the terms of filial and parental love.

As well as being constantly returned to the family nexus by these traditional *double entendres*, we can increasingly hear an explicit working over of filial feelings in popular songs. This is probably because pop music in its present form has now been with us long enough for numbers of its devotees to have reached 'middle' if not 'old' age. Too many people have stubbornly refused to grow out of it, and have tried instead to make it grow with them, finding in it the new emotional resonances and reflections of later life, including those linked to the experience of parenting and to re-evaluations of one's own parents. In the hugely popular music of Bruce Springsteen there is a strong preoccupation with the father–son relationship. The work of blues-oriented musicians such as Eric Clapton inclines more towards images of the mother, as we might expect given the roots of blues in most profound experiences of separation and loss. In the last part of this chapter, and in the next, there are closer examinations of the

oeuvres of these two, as providing particularly rich examples
of the psychosocial meanings of popular music.

As Judith Williamson (1990) has suggested, pop music –
even of the 'light' variety much despised by the intelligentsia –
may do valuable psychological work in our culture in the
consistent expression it gives to basic emotional need, to the
yearnings of the 'heart'. To understand the full depth of its
appeal one should remember that 'the first cut is the deepest'
– that in all later relationships people are trying both to
recreate the loves and to recover from the losses of early life.

THE GREAT PRETENDER

The oedipal conflict, as described by Freud, is often thought
of as being about sexual rivalry: at the centre of it is the
child's wish to displace the same-sex parent in union with the
opposite-sex parent. While this dimension is vital to our
overall understanding of the significance of this conflict, we
also need to see it as a key stage in the separation struggle.
In accepting that it cannot take the place of the same-sex
parent, and thereby resolving the conflict through a crucial
renunciation of its wishes, the child is acknowledging the
otherness of its parents, and letting them get on with their
relationship. It is accepting a deeply unpleasurable aspect of
reality – its own lack of power over others – and so taking a
big step towards establishing itself as a securely separate
individual in a social world over which it has little control.
There are some resources to hand to assist the child in this
massive task, the chief of which is the love between the child
and the same-sex parent, with whom some strong identification must take place if the required renunciation is to be
possible. The idea that this identification is achieved entirely
or mainly through fear is typical of potted summaries of
Freud, but is not the understanding within psychoanalysis
itself, where there is often quite a strong emphasis on the
importance of love.

The oedipus complex is then a psychic configuration of
great ambivalence, in which rivalrous aggression (and the
more general hatred of the other which lies behind it) is
released within a most deep attachment. They are respectively
the negative and positive components of the process of
separation. The rivalry provides the necessary experience of

difference and distance; the attachment provides the experience – equally necessary for separation – of a loving other
who can be internalised as a formative element of the
emergent self.

As we have noted, pop music is obviously expressive of the
negative, rejecting side of separation, but were it to do only
this it would have little value in helping those who consume it
to work through the conflicting feelings involved, which means
inhabiting both sides, giving each their due weight – and
hopefully arriving at some complex overall configuration of
feeling in which the aggression is recognised but contained
within the dominant good feelings.

In 1952, after the death of her husband, a Mrs Spector
arranged that his gravestone would bear the inscription 'To
know him was to love him'. Ten years later Mr Spector's son
Phil, on the way to becoming one of the most famous of
record producers and songwriters and to having a profound
influence on the whole development of modern pop, wrote a
song for a girl group (the Teddy Bears) which he based
around this inscription. Thus in the relatively early days of
post-war pop music a man's positive feelings about his father
were transmuted into a girl's love for her boy in the lyrics and
the affective heart of a hit song. But on the surface pop
music was at that time fairly empty of good feelings about
fathers.

There was however a famous piece of idealised paternal
imagery used in talking about the most famous and emblematic of all pop stars: Elvis Presley was 'the King'. Elaine
Dundy's remarkable double biography (1985) of Gladys (his
mother) and Elvis Presley throws light on the origins of
Presley's king-liness, and its relationship to the crisis of
masculinity. Such a crisis was then gathering in the post-war
world, although the surface of popular culture may have still
been peopled largely by untroubled men of Hollywood and of
the workingmen's club. In Dundy's account, it is poignant and
ironic that a man whose own father was anything but kingly
should become known to millions as the King; this came
about because Elvis was a king to his mother. The mother's
passion for her son, and his reflection of that in the development of his public self, came to resonate with and flood an
entire culture.

While Phil Spector spoke through the Teddy Bears and
through a lyric of cosy adolescent love of his feelings for his

father, Gladys Presley spoke through her son, and through
the public adulation of him, of her feelings for the father and
husband she never had. Both her father and husband were
unambitious casual labourers, handsome, gentle and loving
men, but men without energy, will or power, poor 'white
trash' who could not provide adequately for their families. The
man that Gladys wished to create in her son, and that
millions of people found in him, was not only handsome,
gentle and loving, but an embodiment of power. This was a
power of various kinds. It was a power of money, the power
to be secure, to be able to provide and to give to others, a
power which Elvis so acutely lacked in his early life. It was
also a sexual power, and an artistic power, the power to
move, to evoke feelings and identifications. Shaped thus by
his mother's needs, and swept along by the burgeoning
economic and cultural significance of youth, Presley in his sad
ending could only confirm how disastrous it is to vault from
boyhood to be King, without the chance to build up any inner
selfhood. By the time he died, masculinity was in trouble at
many levels, and the ideals which he had earlier embodied
might have seemed as if they could exist only in a make-
believe world of 1950s movies.

Powerful images in popular culture, however, have an
increasing tendency to keep coming back. Fifties styles
became popular again in the 1980s, and remain so today,
and at deeper levels in pop music itself the legacy of rock
and roll, and especially of its 'King', is still being worked
through. In the post-war period popular music has evolved
into a more complex form, capable of dealing more produc-
tively and directly with emotional struggles. Neither Presley
nor, probably, Spector had the resources, cultural or personal, to work through the oedipal struggle to a resolution
whereby the son achieves some reconcilation with the father
against whom he had to fight to define himself, but from
whom he has also eventually drawn a positive sense of
being a man. In the music they produced there is not even
a direct recognition of this struggle. Spector's magnificent
'wall of sound' facilitated the general emergence of the
female voice in pop, and somehow caught – through the
voice of the adolescent girl – the yearning and the euphoria
characteristic of the separation struggle. But his path was
oblique to the oedipal conflict, oscillating between a childish
sentimentality and the promotion of the powerful sexuality

of the 'girl groups' to whose rise he made a major contribution.

Presley antagonised millions of fathers through his effect
on their sons (and daughters), but – with no effective father
to struggle against – was not himself engaged in an effective
struggle with his father. He was his mother's phantasy answer
to the question of what a man is. He was a clean-cut boy who
said 'Yes Sir'. The 1960s of course did away with all that sort
of deference, and so set the wider cultural stage for pop
music to move on emotionally and deal more directly with
oedipal issues. In this and other ways it was then able to
become more fully the sort of cultural institution which this
book is about, able at least in parts of its output to function
as a resource for emotional integration. Presley's music may
have been able to function in that way, but almost in spite of
Elvis himself, who was a pretender – though splendid and
poignant in his pretence – to the achievements of manhood.

THE BOSS AND HIS FATHER

As an example of a later musician who marks how things
have moved along, we can take Bruce Springsteen. In view of
the preceding discussion he is a particularly appropriate
example, blending as he has done in a self-conscious way
strong elements of both Presley and Spector, both clear,
jumping rock and roll and a dense, moving barrage of sound.

In British writing about rock there is little exploration of
the significance of Springsteen's work, though an unconsid-
ered enjoyment of his music may be admitted to. Modish
cultural commentary has been more attentive to the decon-
structors of gender. Springsteen's outspoken, conventional
masculinity may seem like a hangover from the pre-feminist
era of rock, something which can only be a sham now that
the old certainties of gender have dissolved. That process of
dissolution has to some extent been led by developments in
pop music, and it has been enacted more by men than by
women. Masculinity became a focal point of cultural decomposition, a process represented most clearly by men in rock
who were subverting the codes of heterosexual difference.
(Ironically, the visibility of this collapse of masculinity may
have been due in part to the generally greater prominence of
men in the music industry.) More recently the interest in

Madonna as icon, and in her manipulations of sexual imagery, has moved the spotlight away from gay and transvestite men.

To receive much attention from cultural critics during a period when cultural criticism has been preoccupied with signs, musicians have probably needed to be concerned themselves with their own sign-values. One who is not particularly conspicuous or innovative at that level may then be mistaken for a simple recidivist, which to some extent has been Springsteen's fate. But the masculinity he represents carries more than just the formal signs of the masculine stereotype – voice, dress, postures and so on. Those alone, when deployed with the intensity which he commands, might lead to the kind of narcissistic hyper-masculine strutting of which rock has many examples. Springsteen's importance is that he revives a positive moral content to those masculine forms. One might venture the observation that his music is authentic – without sentimentality and without excess.

Setting aside the rather adolescent, contrivedly allegorical style of his first two albums, he has consistently explored a set of moral themes in his songs. There is a morality of place, of home town, sometimes expressed in sad reflections on the post-industrial loss of community (hence his well-known dona-tion to the striking British miners in 1984). And there is a morality of emotional responsibility and commitment, of 'Ties That Bind'. Specifically, this is about assuming the masculine responsibilities of husband and father. Nonetheless, alongside this assumption of responsibility there is another set of masculine roles being vigorously lived out in the music, those associated with the imagery of fast cars, good times and rock and roll.

Thus overall a complete male trajectory from exuberant youth to responsible parent is encompassed, and is estab-lished as continuous – Springsteen has basically one voice, though he speaks in several different age registers. The epic excitement of the young man's music is not lost in the songs of maturity, while in even the most beltingly euphoric num-bers and the songs of rebellion there is often a sense of complexity and of the consequences that follow in life. 'Racing in the Street', for example, turns out to be a very melancholic song of disenchantment.

The music adds up to a statement that the received forms of masculinity can still support a coherent mode of being, organised around moral concerns. And it is a nurturant mode

– nowhere here is there any of the ambivalence towards or
contempt for women that enters the work of some other rock
lyricists of comparable talent. Women in Springsteen's songs
are partners, whether in pleasure, achievement or tragedy,
and they are to be cared for without condescension. This
consciousness has its limits; the social and ecological costs of
cars, for example, do not come into it. Its strength is in its
sensitivity to a range of ordinary moral struggles. Within the
vocabulary of masculinity Springsteen finds terms of empathy,
generosity and citizenship, and uses them to engage with the
difficulties of leading a satisfying life. This effort is frequently
portrayed as unsuccessful – for example insofar as stable
manual employment helped to underpin the masculine identity, then that identity is not recoverable in the same form in
post-industrial settings, and the beleaguered man may be
firmly on the 'Downbound Train'.

But identity does not, at its deepest level, need daily
reinforcement from specific social roles. The roots of masculine identity are familial, and the present crisis of masculinity
is an expression of a crisis of family relationships. In a
number of Springsteen's songs there are references to another
dimension of the masculine developmental trajectory, that
from the youth's struggles with his father to some resolution
of the intergenerational conflict and to a father–son reconciliation. For this to happen, the son has to feel some gratitude,
and to see the father with some compassion. Springsteen-
as-son achieves this with images of his father as worn and
damaged by a lifetime's labour, or as demeaned by relative
poverty ('Factory' and 'Used Cars', where these images occur
strongly, are two of his most exquisite songs). A familiar
tragedy is that this compassionate rediscovery of the father
comes too late, perhaps after the father's death, and the men
have to live and die with their guilt unalleviated – 'Our sins
lie unatoned' ('My Father's House'). But given at least the
wish to make good, to forgive and be forgiven, then the son
has arrived at a mature moral capacity, on the basis of which
concerns for others, and for the wider community, can
develop.

As noted earlier, some popular renderings of psychoanalytic theory have suggested that it is the son's fear of
the father which is the basis for identification with him (the
so-called 'castration complex'), so that masculine identity is
seen as conveyed from one generation to another along a

line of terror. Stepping into the father's shoes is the son's escape from subjugation. Springsteen's music illustrates an alternative understanding: that masculinity is achieved through a predominantly loving identification, through a reparative and regretful approach to the father. Of course this does not produce a 'happy ending'. The son still has to find his way – 'I didn't think there'd be so many steps I'd have to take on my own' ('Walk Like a Man'), and may remain vulnerable to surges of oedipal anxiety (as in 'I wish I were blind' – though even in this powerful song about sexual jealousy the overall mood is distinctly mournful rather than aggressively rivalrous). But the basis has been laid for a positive inhabiting of the father's role.

Whether his particular personal history has clearly followed the pattern of conflict and reconciliation is not primarily the issue. It seems (for example from the limited material on Springsteen's family in Dave Marsh's otherwise detailed book on the man) as if Springsteen senior was a hard-working man but unsuccessful in the sense that the family were never able to feel that they were a part of American affluence, as he moved from one poorly paid job to another. '"My mother is the great energy – she's the energy of the show," Bruce said' (Marsh, 1987, p. 86). Significantly, his mother was a great Elvis fan. Yet, unlike Vernon Presley, Doug Springsteen must somehow have provided his son with enough powerful experience of fathering, both oppressive and loving, to fuel his long creative engagement with masculinity.

In any case, from the point of view of cultural analysis, what matters more than the fit between biography and art is the imaginative expression given to some of the trials and possibilities of modern masculinity. A story Springsteen has told at live performances, included on the live album set, does though locate his own experience very clearly in this context. He tells of bitter conflicts with his father during his long-haired, guitar-playing 1960s adolescence, and of how his father looked forward to the army 'making a man of him'. The story ends delicately on his father's expression of relief on hearing that Bruce had failed his medical and could not be sent to Vietnam. At such moments of reparation the son discovers the father's love for him, and his own for his father.

His father has been present in his performances not only in these anecdotes and reminiscences to the audience but also symbolically in the form of Clarence Clemons, the large black saxophonist of Springsteen's E Street Band. Springsteen's stage relationship with Clemons was one of excited admiration: 'Come on, big man!' 'Do I have to say his name?... Weighing in at 260 pounds!' 'Big man, assist me please.' The big daddy on tenor is an object of affection and respect, yet his powerful musical voice is deployed within a framework set by Springsteen, who is 'the Boss'. This at least is how the music press has sometimes referred to him, and it is in a way an appropriate title in that the young man becomes the master of his internalisations, and acquires (whether as person, artist or both) an authority. This is not of course a masculine prerogative, and the resonance and sureness of Springsteen's singing particularly recalls that of Bessie Smith, but it comes about in a particular way for the man. The father's voice is deeply contested but finally valued, and appears in the son's mature expression as an exciting and potent force now harnessed to the son's project.

Looked at this way, the current crisis of masculinity is about fathers and sons finding it impossible to forgive each other, resulting in the sons' refusal to inherit the fathers' masculine identities, and their failure to reproduce masculinity as a moral resource. In the terms of some forms of anti-sexism, that failure may be welcomed as a defeat for patriarchal relations. But for Bruce Springsteen's massive, cross-class audience, the reassertion of masculinity as a worthwhile and feasible project is compelling music, for both men and women. That his audience is generally white may suggest that black people have less need of this kind of reassertion, though it seems more likely that Springsteen, despite his inclusive synthesising of many of the traditions of pop, has been limited by the historical racialisation of the music – both classic rock and roll and the Spector sound appealed mainly to whites. Other developments in pop have tended to separate aesthetic from ethnic distinctions, or at least to blur the lines of racialised division between styles. There is no reason to expect that some such divisions will not persist, but we might hope that future major figures of popular music – and the emotional experiences they can offer – will not be heavily tied to ethnically defined audiences. Perhaps this is where a preoccupation with subverting the existing cultural categories could be especially important and productive.

8   PAIN IN THE SUBURBS

'WONDERFUL RUBBISH'

In any attempt to talk or to write seriously about pop music, as in the previous chapter, one risks bringing a certain kind of ridicule upon oneself.[1] 'Don't be pretentious', some people will say, or think. 'Pop music is trivial, even though it may be great fun. Don't presume it to have a meaning or an importance which it doesn't.' In an admonition of this sort, Simon Hoggart (1990) singles out Eric Clapton as the idol of the '"rock is art" brigade'. Hoggart quotes some rather banal lines from a song Clapton recorded to show how absurd it is to pretend that pop music may be anything more than 'wonderful rubbish'. (The article as a whole was written in fond memory of Del Shannon, who certainly did produce some very wonderful rubbish.)

That particular song will be commented on shortly, but it will be clear that the previous chapter, and this one, offer precisely the kind of analysis that Hoggart and others find ridiculous. This is done in the uncomfortable awareness that the dangers to which they draw attention are very real. Some 'rock' criticism may easily betray an incapacity to separate the writer's own enthusiasms and antipathies from the aims of social analysis. Let us hope that such mistakes are not made here.

SHAPES OF PAIN

By most standards Eric Clapton has led a distressed life.[2] In the last few years he seems to have achieved some kind of stability – he is now forty-seven years old, and is reported to have had analysis – but prior to that there was a long history of disturbance. However, psychoanalysis teaches that lived distress is not the same thing as psychic pain. On the contrary it posits that under some circumstances there is an inverse relation between the two. It is the incapacity to tolerate psychic pain which is seen as the source of the symptoms and the acting-out, the alcoholism and addiction, the manipulativeness and so on, which are the forms of or the occasions for the felt distress. In Clapton's case there has presumably been enough of a capacity to endure pain to have ensured that he has stayed alive to the present, and has furthermore remained creative. It will be argued that this capacity has been expressed in some of his musical output, which can therefore offer to the listener some containment of painful feelings. Further, the mass popularity of such music suggests that mass culture may not be all bad news, psychologically speaking – that we may find it offers some containment of psychic pain, and that it thereby fosters endurance as well as evasions.

We will not engage in a psychobiographical study of Clapton; there is not enough reliable information about the man in the public domain to do so. Nonetheless it is worth mentioning in passing some relevant details; they are consistent with the theme, even if they do not explain anything. One crucial element in Eric Clapton's biography is that he was in effect abandoned by his parents. He never knew his father, a Canadian serviceman stationed in England, and his mother left him at the age of two to be brought up by her mother and stepfather in a very working-class home in a Surrey village, in the days when there still were working-class homes in Surrey villages. (She married another serviceman and went to live in Germany.) We would expect this early life situation to exacerbate the normal developmental phenomena of both rage and idealisation felt towards the primal mother and towards woman in general.

It is easy to document these themes in Clapton's musical output, and also in his personal life. A tide of rage, often self-destructive, has borne Clapton along for much of his life, as his near-fatal over-use of alcohol and his three- or four-year period of drug addiction in the early 1970s suggest. But in his early teens he found that music could be a container for some of this rage. Observers have often commented on the sometimes angry quality of his guitar technique. His one-time nickname 'Slowhand' referred to the good-natured slow handclap which in his early years of blues club playing was his fans' response during the frequent intervals when he had to replace a guitar string broken by the force of his playing. There is an undertow of contained fury in his best-known piece of music: 'Layla', a song written both in anguish and in pleading about and to Patti Harrison, who was at that time rejecting Clapton's overtures to her.

The counterpoint to the rage is the image of the idealised woman, the replacement for the lost mother and – more than a replacement – a barrier against the rage and hatred felt for the mother who failed. This idealisation is nowhere better expressed in Clapton's work than in his exquisite song 'You Look Wonderful Tonight'. The romantic love song is as integral to Clapton's work as it is to popular music generally, and this is one of the finest examples of the genre. It is not however typical, either of Clapton or of the discourse of love in pop music as a whole. More often the story is one of lost love, and although a sense of anger is often part of the lament, the predominant affect – as indeed it is in 'Layla' – is yearning.

So romantic idealisation is not the main way in which in his music Clapton deals with the problem of the mother who rejected him. In many songs he is able to confront fairly directly the sense of loss and desolation, more perhaps in his music than he has been able to sustain successfully in much of his life. It is this capacity for examining his inner landscape of loss which marks Clapton out from any other British musician.

The best tracks on his albums are usually either his versions of blues standards, or his own songs. He is not a prolific writer, but over the years has produced a substantial number of memorable songs in which this self-examination is pursued. Consider as one example 'Holy Mother', from the 1987 LP *August*. This was written in memory of a friend of his who committed suicide – another heroin addict, Richard Manuel of the American group The Band. Clapton is here still appealing to some all-powerful and all-good mother to rescue him from despair, but overall the song conveys little hope that the appeal will be met: 'Holy Mother, where are you?'

As a boy, Clapton was apparently a rather solitary character who spent hours drawing. He was still interested enough in art in his late teens to start at art school, but by then he had found a far more effective way of creating the shapes in which many of his feelings could find expression, and some containment – the aural shapes of blues phraseology. His main influence has continued to be blues, and his significance as a musician rests on his translation of blues into some of the varied forms which comprise contemporary popular music.

This translation is sometimes direct, sometimes very loose. He has not added to the basic emotional language of blues, but has made that language of loss into the vernacular of many people far removed from the social origins of blues. The major contention here is therefore that important, integrative psychic work is daily done in the consumption of such popular music. In the rest of this chapter we will look more closely at this phenomenon, probing it in one or two different directions.

HOLDING ON

Clapton describes blues as the first love of his life. For a long time during and after his adolescence he regarded it as his mission in life to protect 'this beautiful music'. He left the Yardbirds in 1965 just as they were beginning to find fame and fortune because he did not want to play the kind of eclectic pop music that they were beginning to. The following year, after joining the John Mayall Bluesbreakers because they did provide a setting within which his commitment to blues could be expressed, he left them as well because he had come to find their allegiance to the blues too formulaic. He wanted to explore new ways in which blues affect could be worked upon musically. (Admittedly at times since Clapton himself has also produced rather repetitive music by turning the handle on the blues machine, but every so often – and particularly since the mid-1980s – a surge of creativity has carried him beyond this.)

One could say that 'this beautiful music' is psychically the equivalent of a woman. Overall, Clapton's career presents a picture of great fidelity to a sensual, truthful blues-woman.[3] He describes a particular bluesy tone on the guitar as 'that woman tone'. When battling with his addiction and full, we might imagine, of feelings of internal badness, he felt that to pick up his guitar and play blues on it would be an 'insult' to the music (Turner, 1976), a contamination of the idealised woman. If blues is – in part, and at a certain level – a woman, then blues-based music is not only the medium through which the lost maternal object is mourned and commemorated. Also it is itself the lost object, the maternal body. It is both the

voice of mourning, that is a *subject*, and also a compelling
object of desire. This duality is similar to the dual nature of
the mother herself; like her, blues is both the containing
space and the sensual field, both environment and object to
use Winnicott's distinction again (see Chapter 5).[4]

At the centre of blues is the guitar, which again is both
voice and object. We hear it wailing and, in the words of the
George Harrison song which Clapton recorded with the
Beatles, it 'gently weeps'. At the same time the guitar very
clearly represents the female body, caressed and admired,
over which men weep.

The primal object is of course not always adored and good;
both music and instrument also appear as bad objects. There
is that 'Mean old blues', and, indeed, 'Mean woman blues'.
And there was the curious practice of guitar smashing, of
which Eric Clapton was never an exponent. It seems that he
was sufficiently able to convert rage into sound, to get his
guitar to respond adequately to his feeling. Jimi Hendrix, one
of the few musicians who can be compared with Clapton,
could not. It seems that for Hendrix the intractable otherness
of the guitar was intolerable, and it had therefore to be
destroyed. I would understand this to be one reason for his
early death, while Clapton is still with us.[5] So, as well as the
idealisation of the object, we have the anger and the despair
felt towards it. After all, 'blues' are bad feelings. That they are
also the source of great excitement, solace and strength
reflects the contradictory passions felt towards the primal
object.

Given this dominance of the maternal matrix, and notwithstanding the secondary phallic role that the guitar can also
obviously play, it is not surprising that blues does not deal
much with the oedipal struggle. Rivalry and jealousy of a
sometimes paranoid intensity is of course a prominent theme
in many old blues verses (and is very marked in the songs of
the contemporary blues musician Robert Cray). However this
is not 'oedipal' material, except at a very primitive level. There
is no ambivalent struggle with a father or friend, no challenge
of responsibility. There is only impersonal hostility towards
the rival, and above all anger and hatred felt towards the
deceiving woman, with panic at the prospect of losing her
bed, food and body.

In this connection we can note George Harrison's observation that Eric, though an old friend, expected him to want to

fight with him after Patti Harrison had left George for Eric. Harrison (perhaps dealing with his own oedipal feelings in the diametrically opposite way) had no such idea, but the primitive quality of Clapton's anxiety in this area may help to explain the attraction to him of the very light and ordinary, and crudely oedipal, song of Bob Marley's, which Clapton recorded and had a big hit with in 1974: 'I shot the sheriff' – the song that Simon Hoggart used to illustrate his argument; it is hardly representative of Clapton's work.

In Clapton's own songs there are only occasional appeals to a paternal figure, and these very conventional ones, as in the song 'Lord, Give Me Strength' written during his withdrawal from heroin and found on the 1974 LP *461 Ocean Boulevard*. There is also 'Hold Me Lord' from the *Another Ticket* LP of 1981, though here the appeal is actually to a quasi-maternal saviour, on whom a sense of existence depends: 'Hold me Lord, I'm slipping through, Hold me tight, I beg of you'. These words direct us to the powerful preoccupation in the whole blues tradition with the imagery of 'holding'. One of my own favourite examples of this is a B.B. King track called 'Hold On'. From Clapton we also have it in another track from the *August* LP, again called 'Hold on'. We need only a little psychoanalytic imagination to see what it is that must be held on to: the loving presence of the other, the precious object, the mother's body, or – as Clapton simply puts it – 'the feeling'.

Blues then is a woman, in the sense of being a creative evocation and embodiment of a desired object, as well as an artistic deployment of a containing medium. Its containing function resides in the ways in which it is recognised in the music that the cry to 'hold on' is a vain one – the songs in which this imagery occurs are usually deeply mournful ones, coloured heavily by a sense of fading and slipping away.[6] They are reality principle songs, 'narratives of love and loss' in the Rustins' phrase. As such, they can signal a rediscovery of the good internal object which was built in remembrance of the lost mother, and is her legacy. Thus from the pain of loss a sense of well-being can emerge, a work of restoration amid the ruins. We can take this to be one formulation of the healing power of tragic art.

The restorative moment is not explicit in blues songs, the words of which are often quite paranoid,[7] but is somehow there in the forms and timbres of the music. At the centre of the aesthetic encounter with blues is the sense of reclamation, of rediscovering an internal resource.[8] Speaking of his first hearings of blues musicians, Clapton has said:

> I wanted what they were experiencing, I wanted to know where they got it from, what it was all about, and it seemed to strike something in me that was rearing its head. I still don't know what that is, but it's a drive to express something, and that seemed to me the most ideal or the most beautiful way of expressing something. ('The Journeyman', Radio 1, January 1990.)

In understanding Clapton's account, we must also take account here of the element of bohemian identification with the exotic outsider, which underlay the interest of some white youth in black music. But that in turn may stem partly from more primitive sources in the search for the primal object, or rather – if the analysis of blues adopted here is correct – in the struggle to acknowledge its loss.

In one received understanding of art, some distance is required between the life experience of the artist and the content of the art work – that is, the latter should not be simply autobiographical, unless explicitly so. The symbolic and therapeutic power of art depends, according to this way of thinking, on the extent to which the artist has reworked his or her feelings and resymbolised them, reflected on them from the viewpoints of others and located them in cultural traditions. Through these processes the artist's feelings can become more contained, and their (mediated) expression in the artwork can offer more containment. However the wrong kind of reworking can result in too great a distance from authentic experience, and therefore in clichés, sentimentality, intellectualisation or rationalisation.

Blues-based popular music may be seen to suffer from both of these problems of distance. It was a feature of blues (perhaps in common with many other folk arts with relatively small audiences) that the singers put themselves and their experiences quite directly into their songs. The meaning of this kind of personal statement, to both singer and audience, is likely to be different when it is being broadcast on MTV. On the other hand, blues is also readily experienced as a relatively limited set of schematic and easily clichéd musical forms, perhaps of a kind well suited for inclusion in the 'sentimental' vocabulary of popular music.

Of course it is not always clear what is meant by sentimentality. As a rough and ready definition we could take it to mean the use of an expressive idiom which short-circuits the toleration and exploration of feelings, by offering a stylised and closed way of apprehending them. It has been said in criticism of some of Clapton's music that it is sentimental, particularly the song he wrote about the death of his young son (killed in an accidental fall from the window of the apartment where he lived with his mother). Some of the words of this song ('beyond the door, there's peace I'm sure ... there'll be no more tears in heaven') do seem to offer the clichéd idealisation of death characteristic of some everyday forms of 'sentimentality' (though not characteristic, incidentally, of blues). We may also be uncomfortable with the public way in which Clapton has chosen to process his feelings of grief, by their expression in this song and its performance.

It might then be said that here is an example of the way in which a popular cultural artefact may not quite manage to provide an effective containment of feelings, acting instead in part as a device for bleeding them of some authenticity (through manic or sentimental denial, or some other means). Is Clapton in 'Tears in Heaven' both too close to and too far from his own experience? One should be wary of passing such a judgment from the comfortable position of not having had that particular kind of grief to contend with. We could however note that the parents of James Bulger (a toddler abducted and murdered by two older boys) decided to have this music at the boy's funeral. If it can help people in such circumstances to tolerate the unbearable, then perhaps it has some powerful psychocultural value, whatever reservations we may have about the words of the song. It is after all a typical complaint of the elite that the common people are sentimental.

MODERNITY AND MOURNING

It is beyond our means here to discuss in any depth why the particular forms of blues music are so apposite – even without lyrics – for the expression of feelings of grief and resignation, nor why this most powerful modern expression of mourning

should have been developed so distinctively by black people
in the southern United States in the inter-war years. We can
speculatively link it with the theme of separation in popular
music (see Chapter 7), this time on the socio-historical level,
and suggest that as a musical form blues is an expression of
the massive historical experience of the traumatic separation
of modern slavery (separation from original home, and then
from the possibility of secure attachments in slave society). It
is a reflection, from the vantage point of (imposed) modernity
and separateness, back upon that experience of loss, as
represented or re-enacted mainly in the experience of sexual
relationships.

We may then link the emergence of present forms of popular
music influenced by blues to the development of modern
culture as a whole, and see them as an expression of the
'separation' which modernity represents. At the heart of the
everyday experience of modernity has been an experience of
separation and loss, separation from the nexus of values and
social institutions which we moderns believe to have existed in
an earlier time, and the loss of some innocent or wholesome
state. Whether or not there is any historical truth in this
experience is not the point; it is sufficient that we *experience*
modernity as being premissed upon, or as consisting of an
endless series of, radical separations from sources of value and
stability. The structures of blues are one way we have appropriated and developed of containing the anxieties thus generated.

It would be an interesting exercise in cultural history to
pursue this thesis in one specific context, and to establish
why R&B, the urbanised form of the blues, took such a
hold on an important section of youth culture in Britain in
the 1960s, and why consequently it was through a British
experience that this musical influence then spread across
the world, having an enormous impact as it did on the now
global development of popular music. Numbers of mainly
working and lower middle class young men, congregating
around British art schools in the early 1960s, enacted a
cultural revolution, inserting the affective language of blues
into the everyday culture of advanced capitalism (and there-
after most of the rest of the world). Simon Frith and
Howard Horne's discussion of British pop music (1990)
highlights the fusion of cultural impulses which it embodied,
and how pop drew upon art school traditions to dissolve the
art versus commerce distinction, but they do not address

the question of why the blues was selected – from among a
number of bohemian alternatives – as such a significant
model of authenticity. We might speculate that there were
particular resonances between the passions of the blues and
the crises of masculinity which these young men were living
through, as the first post-war generation walked suburban
streets and town centres stricken with adolescent longings
and modern loneliness.

But here we shall simply have to observe, as William
Willeford (1985) puts it, that 'the blues is an extraordinary
development in the education of the heart'.

In the previous chapter's discussion of the music of Bruce
Springsteen, it was suggested that it presented a coherent and
positive model of modern masculinity. The present discussion
of Clapton can also be read in this way. His resolution of the
crisis of masculinity is very different from Springsteen's (and
probably less secure), but both are attempts to inhabit the
pains of contemporary manhood. Clapton's, however, is
grounded much more strongly in the affective domain of the
blues, and does not therefore reach into the concerns with
authority, personal responsibility and citizenship which are
the stuff of many of Springsteen's oedipal, more outward-
looking songs.

In contrast to the constant struggle for maturity of a
Springsteen, blues-based music may sometimes be emotionally regressive, but there is nonetheless in Clapton's work
and in other contemporary derivatives of blues a persistent
concern with emotional reality. At one level, given the
paucity of women blues-oriented musicians, this concern is
predominantly with the dependency needs and the grieving
at the core of masculine identity. But whatever the reasons
for the gender imbalance among musicians there is no
doubt about the un-gendered appeal of the music. Whatever
sociologically specific route an artist may take to the
depressive position, its achievement can be appreciated by a
very diverse audience, at least within certain broad cultural
limits.

Of course even the best popular music may be appropriated by unintegrated states of mind. Some other post-R&B
developments in pop music, taking their cues more from the
Rolling Stones and the later Yardbirds rather than from
Clapton, have translated 'bluesy' sounds into rather narcissistic languages of musical performance. (Readers will be

left to guess which types of music are referred to here, in keeping with the undertaking made at the start of the previous chapter to avoid sectarian claims.) The potential for painful working-through always has to compete with hatred and idealisation.

It cannot be unusual to feel that if it were not for music, one would go mad – would certainly have gone mad as an adolescent, if not later. The cultural availability of blues-based music (though one had to search it out in the early 1960s) provides both a social ratification of feelings of turbulence, pain and desire, and – somewhat mysteriously – an opportunity for aesthetic containment of them. Without this kind of resource, the pain of emotional development may be unbearable.

In the struggle to be sane the main instruments for evoking and containing feelings are the shared forms of expressive cultural activity. It is not obviously the case that popular music is foremost among such cultural forms, partly because of the prejudice that it does not and cannot have emotional depth. However it is a general argument of this book that some quite mundane forms of popular culture may indeed be popular precisely because of the emotional depths at which they engage us. At these depths the social nature of our identities and pleasures is perpetually being reaffirmed, and impulse is being both released, and recalled to reality.

In the kind of music exemplified particularly clearly by Springsteen, sexuality and aggression are vividly conveyed (sometimes explicitly in the lyrics, sometimes implicitly, even subliminally, in the sensual qualities of the music) but marshalled behind the effort to develop or restore good relations with good parental figures, representative of authority and reality.

The example of Clapton takes us from the oedipal level to a more pre-oedipal terrain, to that of the blues rather than Springsteen's synthesis of various American folk and pop traditions. On this terrain the tension is between the regressive yearning for the lost maternal object, and the struggle to confront the reality of that loss. Clapton's mission has been to find musical shapes and textures that can contain the pains of separateness. The process of separation, of acknowledging loss, is the most basic dimension of the tension between the pleasure and reality principles. Emotional development depends upon both a *renunciation* of and mourning for the lost object, and the *installation* of the object, with memories of its gratifying goodness, in the mind. In a sense we have to let go and hold on at the same time, to preserve the matrix of feeling at the same time as we must leave it.

PART III
PROSPECTS

9   WHAT DO THE PEOPLE WANT?

HATE IN THE TRANSFERENCE

We have now reviewed a number of case studies intended
to illustrate the idea that some of the major institutions of
popular culture are important not only as a sociological
phenomenon, in that they are important to millions of
people, but also in their psychological meanings. They
enable us to do positive psychic work in their expression
and containment of fundamental emotional tensions. They
give expression to a range of impulses – libidinal, sensual,
regressive and aggressive – but contain and subordinate
them within an acceptance of social limits, of the otherness
of others, and the inevitability of separation and loss.

This sympathetic view of popular culture having been
derived with the help of psychoanalysis, it would now be
interesting briefly to turn our gaze around, and, instead of
looking psychoanalytically at popular culture, to look at the
place of psychoanalysis in that culture. This is necessarily
an historical exercise, because popular culture is almost by
definition in a state of constant flux, and the meanings
attached to particular ideas or images are constantly being
renegotiated – as is clear if we look at the history of
representations of psychoanalysis that can be found in
different times and places.

Overall we find that popular culture is not nearly as kind
towards psychoanalysis as psychoanalytic ideas have been
towards it in the preceding chapters. When psychoanalysis
first arrived and its presence began to permeate popular
awareness, some highly positive reactions were in evidence.
There is some evidence though that as time went on more
negative and rejecting attitudes began to take hold. This is
an oversimplification as a general characterisation of the
history of attitudes towards psychoanalysis, but there are
certainly some indications in support of it – in historical
studies of the early reception of analysis, and in the picture

we can readily draw of the hostility towards it in many situations in more recent times.[1]

Why might such a shift have occurred? To try and answer this let us look firstly at the quality of the early positive reactions. Two studies by Nathan Hale (1971) and John Burnham (1979) look at two very different cultural sectors, the popular and the avant-garde. In many contexts one might expect these to be very different in the kinds of understandings and values they register. But there are some common elements in the descriptions of how psychoanalysis was appropriated in them, the main one of which is the sense of relief or even liberation which it was felt to bring. Hale (see his Chapter 15) describes types of popular magazine stories in which miracle cures by psychoanalytic methods, sometimes based on an analogy with surgery, were described, or in which the unconscious was welcomed as a 'helpful subliminal self'. Within this understanding, psychoanalysis was a key to a valuable resource. Burnham describes the welcome given to Freud by the bohemian avant-garde for the way in which his ideas were taken to support their iconoclastic attack on 'hypocrisy' about sexual behaviour. We are familiar today with echoes of these understandings of psychoanalysis, in the views that it gives licence to sexual disinhibition or perversity, or is the source of misguided, 'wet' liberal apologies for depravity. Note though that the evaluation is here typically transformed from positive and welcoming into negative and contemptuous.

One might say that there is a sort of manic quality to the earlier reactions, a sort of need to co-opt psychoanalysis into an optimistic view of human nature and of the future for Western culture. It was imagined to be a saving, healing or liberating doctrine. This is also evident in another historical study, Jed Sekoff's (1989) review of some representations of analysis in Hollywood. His examples are somewhat later, so we should not be too precise about the periodisation of any historical thesis, but we can hold to the suggestion that overall in the representations we might find across Western culture of psychoanalysis there was an early preponderance of favourable ones, and a later preponderance of negative ones, in which it is at best regarded as irrelevant and outdated, or is roundly attacked for its lack of scientificity, its preoccupation with sexuality and the bizarre, and – as the last wave of feminist-inspired critique since the 1960s has suggested – is dismissed as an oppressive exercise of patriarchal power.

We could link these phases to broad cultural trends, and see the representations of analysis as consequences of changes taking place across the culture. The philosopher Frank Cioffi has suggested [2] that the reason for its rapid spread and acceptance in the early years of this century (if we accept that it did spread easily, which is not obviously the case) was that it provided a pseudo-scientific rationale for changes in cultural mores that were already happening (for other reasons) – the greater permissiveness and loosening of ties to some traditional cultural authorities that were becoming evident by the 1920s.

Pursuing this possibility, the later turning against psychoanalysis could be understood as being a part of a second wave of cultural loosening and de-traditionalisation which has gathered pace in the second half of this century. An important theme in this development has been the growth of distrust in scientific expertise, and a rejection particularly of those traditionally authoritative forms of knowledge represented by medicine and psychiatry, with which psychoanalysis has, wrongly, been strongly identified.

As analysis has become more unpopular, the space for personal reflection and emotional sensitivity opened up to a large extent by its impact in the early years of this century has been colonised by the humanistic psychologies, one particularly strong appeal of which has been the downplaying of expert knowledge. The rejection of the conceptual and technical intricacies of psychoanalysis, and the affirmation of the self-transformative powers of the individual, are clearly more congenial to a culture with a strong streak of narcissism (though see Chapter 10) than is a practice in which the interpretive activity of someone else is a vital part of the therapeutic encounter.

So we could develop on these lines a socio-cultural explanation for the waxing and waning of the fortunes of psychoanalysis in the wider culture. We can however also add to it a more psychodynamically grounded account of what has been going on by seeing the early positive representations as a sort of manic denial of the basic message which Freud was bringing, which is not that we can and should be sexually liberated (though psychoanalysis certainly does say that we need not be sexually immiserated), but that we are inevitably deeply disappointed and disenchanted creatures, and that we are bound in the core of our psyches to the needs of others.

Psychoanalysis has developed a rich vocabulary to describe how the psyche is based on internalisations of others. The centrality of loss and disenchantment to emotional development is a theme in Freud's work, though one often overlooked, and becomes manifestly a central principle in Klein and some other post-Freudian traditions. Viewed this way, psychoanalysis is a reminder to all who encounter it of our fundamental relatedness to others and our basically conflicted and disappointed nature. As time went on and this core insight became more clearly and securely a part of the analytic tradition, and psychoanalysis became more differentiated from other forms of psychological thought, it became harder to overlook the attitude of resignation which analysis enjoins on us, and harder to maintain a manic, superficial welcoming of Freud as one of the saviours brought by modern psychology. (Psychoanalysis emerged during roughly the same short period of time as other schools of psychology, and for many people inside as well as outside this new discipline some of the differences between paradigms took time to crystallise.)

My suggestion is that the venom and contempt with which it has latterly often been treated can be understood as a defensive attempt to annihilate or expel the knowledge of human limitation – a sort of killing of the messenger.

Moreover, at the level of cultural symbols, in this age of the disempowerment of many traditional authorities, psychoanalysis (especially in the image of Freud as bearded, grim, bourgeois, Victorian patriarch) has become the focus for some free-floating fear and hatred of authority. The force of this hatred, and its readiness to express itself, are familiar to many people who have been involved in teaching about psychoanalysis to students who have not elected to study it, such as undergraduates on psychology and social science courses, and health and welfare professionals in training. It is there, ready and waiting, in the minds of students who have never actually read anything by Freud or any other analytic writer, but who are confident that they know what it is about and how little evidence there is for it (Richards, 1994).

These two antipathies towards psychoanalysis – as a reminder of the otherness of reality, and as an embodiment of authority – are connected, psychodynamically, in that authority is a refractory and powerful form of otherness, and is also the form, in the persons of parents, in which otherness is most forcefully represented to us in infancy. Of course this kind of explanation of the unpopularity of psychoanalysis is especially enraging to its critics, since it employs analytic thought to discredit them, and understands their motives as psychopathologies rather than as intellectual missions. We are saying, in effect, that there is a major negative *transference* (see Chapter 2) towards psychoanalysis, a tendency to interpret it in a preconceived way and so to shut out or distort what it might be saying to us. Its ideas about sexuality are overemphasised and banalised, its methods traduced, and its internal development ignored (though in its dogmatic and reductionist tendencies it has indeed given some hooks for these misrepresentations to hang on).

In the domains of popular experience which have been the main concern of this book, things are not as bad nor as definite as the foregoing remarks might suggest. The assassination of Freud has been attempted or desired by many in the intellectual classes, but for the majority with less investment in ideas the indifference to Freud is probably no greater nor less than to any other person of ideas. However the increasing presence of psychology and social science in the increasing number of professional trainings, and the expansion of higher education especially in the humanities and social sciences have meant that ever larger numbers of people are having to take some stock of psychoanalysis, in relation to their work, themselves or their wider understanding of the world. Despite the strong growth of sympathetic interest in it over the last decade, and the consequent emergence of psychoanalytic studies, it cannot be said that psychoanalysis – in the sense of a readiness to explore the complexities of unconscious motivation – has a lot of popular support; the influence of the negative transference is too strong.

This is of relevance to the central theme of this book. Elsewhere (Richards, 1989) I have argued that the reception given to psychoanalysis tells us something important about our culture, about its inability to absorb fully the blows to narcissism implied by the analytic understanding of human development. Accepting the other-ness of others and the intractability of social constraints, at the same time as recognising our dependence on others, are the basic tasks of individual emotional development, according to this understanding. The discomfort involved in this, the 'unease in culture' as Freud called it, is not easily tolerated, but can be by a well-enough individual or culture.

In the preceding chapters we have seen how a variety of popular cultural practices seem to embody or to facilitate the toleration of reality, even to enhance it. Can this be characteristic of a culture which by other indices is not very good at tolerating reality? To extend the question way beyond the vicissitudes of psychoanalysis, we may ask whether such basically healthy forms of cultural participation as have been described could really exist in a culture as unhealthy as ours seems to be so much of the time. It has been suggested that deep currents of pleasure flow through the acceptance of reality and of social membership, but is there not too much need for illusion and too much selfishness and privatisation for this to happen on any large scale in contemporary society, let alone for integrative and reality-based practices to be culturally dominant?

HOW MUCH IS ENOUGH?

The next and final chapter will take up this question. As a way of elaborating on it, or of trying to bring into focus some of the implications of the preceding chapters for our understanding of the overall condition of contemporary society, let us consider a 1950 paper by the psychoanalyst Donald Winnicott on the meanings of the word 'democracy'. Winnicott has been referred to a number of times in this work for his psychological ideas, but not yet for his social thought, of which there was little in his writings. However in a series of short papers and talks in the 1950s he did venture forth (more boldy than psychoanalysts usually do) with a number of ruminations on the consequences for society and politics of taking certain psychoanalytic ideas seriously. In this paper he tackles head-on the questions of what is a democracy, and what are the optimum conditions for its development.

It is in many respects a strikingly naive and presumptuous paper, partly retrieved by his opening admission of naivety, though not entirely since some of the presumption is unacknowledged. He is confident that psychoanalytic thinking can address fundamental issues concerning the nature of the political process – indeed that it can *define* 'democracy'. Thus this paper brings into sharp focus some of the issues which arise when we try to use psychoanalysis, albeit in more qualified and contextualised ways than Winnicott does, to understand contemporary society.

Democracy is defined by Winnicott as a society well adjusted to its healthy members (a neat inversion of the usual formulation of individual health in terms of adjustment to society). By 'health' he means 'maturity', both for individual and society. In terms of the everyday meanings of these words this gets us no further; the latter term tells us no more than the former. However in the context of a psychoanalytic theory the implication is that democracies are societies which in some way reflect or express the inclinations of those individuals who have achieved satisfactory resolutions of the key struggles of emotional development. In the present work (as, broadly, for Winnicott) these involve the acceptance and containment of destructiveness, the ability to tolerate reality, and the integration within an at least partly coherent self of impulses, anxieties and constraints.

Such individuals Winnicott believes to be the spontaneous products of 'good, ordinary homes'. This was in keeping with his faith in the natural, built-in abilities of ordinary parents (especially mothers) to be – in his famous phrase – 'good enough' to nurture healthy persons. Accordingly his main recommendation for the strengthening of democratic tendencies in a society is to allow such homes to function without interference, and to give support to those parents who alone might not have the emotional resources to be able to provide good enough parenting but who with help can do so. As a guide to policy this is, to say the least, negotiable, depending on how we chose to define support, and the criteria for giving it.

But in any case the chief interest of Winnicott's paper here lies in the simplistic but provocative way in which he attempts to quantify the problem, by speculating on how many 'mature' individuals there may be in any society, and on how many such people one needs for a democracy to function. He suggests that perhaps only 30 per cent of the British people may fall into this category, but that this minority may be able to carry with them another 20 per cent of the people, who are 'indeterminates' – not in themselves fully in possession of maturity and the 'democratic factor', but open to its influence when represented by sufficient others. This aggregate 50 per cent may then be sufficient to outweigh the various immature, anti-democratic persons and to provide a basis for the functioning of democratic institutions (which can never be effectively imposed on a people among whom there was not sufficient positive desire for them).

It may be swiftly objected that no such audit by head-count of the 'democratic factor' is possible, since this does not reside in individuals but in the political culture and institutions of a society. But the relationships of individuals to these institutions, and to some democratic values, is still a matter for enquiry – and arguably an important one, even if one does not accept the individualistic trend of Winnicott's thinking that sees individuals as the *source*, in some fundamental way, of political structures. And whether we are counting by individuals, or by institutions and cultural practices, it can still be asked if there are thresholds or levels that can be identified in the observed quantities of 'health' or 'maturity' that enable us to say of a culture as a whole that it is or is not healthy or mature, democratic or not.

In this book it has been suggested that a number of the major institutions of popular culture may be 'mature' in that they allow for integration and containment of feelings. The emphasis has generally been on forms of 'mass' culture, such that there will be few people who are not consumers of one or other kind of experience discussed. What is implied about the 'maturity' or 'health' of the individuals who participate in these cultural forms? And has it to be understood (contrary to much psychoanalytically inspired social criticism, and to some second-nature attitudes among the left and liberal intelligentsia – both to be discussed in the next chapter) that modern society is 'OK', at least in parts – and perhaps even in *sufficient* parts to be as a whole defensible, to be *good enough*?

10 THE CENTRE IS PROBABLY HOLDING

WHO IS COMPLAINING?

One notable change during the 1980s in the British political landscape was the movement across the political spectrum of some of the sentiments and stances of cultural conservatism.[1] Before neo-liberalism came to enjoy the influence it did during that decade, we were accustomed to associate laments about the declining moral fabric of the country or of the world generally with the right in one guise or another. Then we became accustomed to hearing those who identify themselves as of the left decry the current morality or lack of it, mainly in expressions of regret or disgust at what is believed to have been the de-moralising impact of neo-liberal doctrines in many social spheres. The containing fabric of community has been torn to shreds, it has been argued, and many traditional decencies and communitarian values have evaporated in the messianic heat of the Thatcherite programme, or been frozen in its cold cynicism. Some may locate the roots as well as the fruits of this process very largely in the recent political past (probably since 1979), while for others (usually of a more academic persuasion) it is simply the latest if not the highest phase in a process intrinsic to the economic and social relations of capitalist modernity itself. Many long-standing social-democratic and Marxist critiques of market relations and their destructive impact upon culture and community appear from this perspective to have been thoroughly vindicated.

Not that the Jeremiahs of the right have in the meantime fallen silent. However the neo-liberal moral agitation is usually designed to speak to and mobilise the presumed moral *majority*. While the moral critic of society on the left is usually bemoaning the absence or dissolution of such a majority, the value *vacuum* at the heart of late capitalism, it is more often assumed from the vantage point of the right that a good,

common morality is slumbering, not absent or destroyed. To
the extent that the Labour Party has entered this debate, it
has to some extent to echo this populism: a faith in the
enduring decency of the majority has to be retained if one is
seeking to form an elected government. Any populist strategy,
of left or right, has to locate the problem of moral degeneracy
in a minority or in some abstract process of government or
culture. In post-religious times one cannot hope to appeal to
people with the argument that they are sinners and should
repent. Yet, as will be described, this is the kind of approach
which psychoanalytically influenced work has tended to offer
to political discourse; it is not surprising that its offers have
not been taken up.

Of course another effect of the 1980s was to render
problematic any characterisation of political positions on a
left–right dimension, or at least to diversify the landscape
such that other dimensions, often based more on particular
issues, have to be taken into consideration in describing any
political outlook or programme. The left–right dimension
continues though to be of major importance in a number of
its traditional articulations; as the *Observer* columnist Melanie
Phillips, an outspoken contributor to recent debates about
public morality, has pointed out, the left wishes to re-invest
government with its moral duties, as expressed most powerfully in the Welfare State, while the right wishes to reaffirm
the moral responsibilities of the citizenry, most particularly
those of the family.

In a recent book on the moral condition of the United
States, the art critic Robert Hughes has distinguished between
two forms of moral absolutism, which correspond in parts to
a left–right distinction. He describes these as two forms of
'PC' – 'Political Correctness' and 'Patriotic Correctness'. In
the British context, the former was first identified for us in
the 1980s in the sober and accurate reporting of the tabloid
press as the 'Loony Left' phenomenon. Whatever links that
reportage may or may not have had with reality, concern
about the dogmatic imposition of absolutist principles derived
from various forms of contemporary radicalism later spread to
many other journalists and figures of very different political
stripes.[2]

Many of the prime examples of this PC have been
American, but we could name some British forms of the same
phenomenon. Of course to list any is to court great contro-

versy. Some may agree that it is a problem in some contexts but not agree that a particular practice is any part of it, while others are not happy with the category as a whole, seeing it as a piece of right-wing or patriarchal mythology, or as a mountain range made out of a few molehills. So there are risks involved even in giving the term itself house room in a discussion such as this. Hughes' book, *Culture of Complaint*, was received primarily as an assault on Political Correctness (and welcomed or dismissed as such), but is actually even-handed in that it offers equal treatment to the Patriotic Correctness that came to enjoy an ascendancy in America during and since Reagan's presidency. This, as Hughes (1993, p. 44) describes one form of it, is 'a putrid stew of gay-bashing, thinly veiled racism and authoritarian populism'. Both PCs, he argues, involve an assault on the public sphere, on the polity as an inclusive discourse within which the democratic process can be optimised and values rationally debated. Under the sway of PC imperatives, debate is clouded with paranoid suspicions, and poisoned by a disastrous combination of an insistence upon victimhood with the conviction of infallibility.

He suggests that these two forms of prescriptiveness, while they are manifestly at odds with each other, have a common root in the Puritan ethic. In relation to art, the sphere with which Hughes is most directly concerned, the Puritan demanded something morally uplifting. Art had to evince the right spiritual qualities, and to maximise these in those who looked upon it. Under the later influence of Romanticism, this spiritual imperative partly transmuted into a therapeutic one. From the standpoint of what Hughes terms the 'therapeutic fallacy', art has to exercise a therapeutic function, for the individual or for society. Thus for the political correctionists, art has to correct the social evils of racism, sexism and so on by searching them out, attacking them and presenting alternatives to them. For the patriotic correctionist, art must reaffirm the allegedly consensual values, and help to renew the moral commitment of each generation to them. Hughes' critique of the two forms of correctness is not a relativistic one. His pitch is for skill and quality in art, and against the primacy of political content. He is for the autonomy of the aesthetic domain, though he recognises at least implicitly that this autonomy is relative, and that art has political meanings.

From Hughes' account we can extrapolate a psychoanalytic

description of these two forms of moral rectitude, which would also stress their underlying similarity. We could see them both as symptomatic of fragile and poorly integrated superego structures. The PC self is one lacking in firmly internalised principles on which to ground itself, and is unable to confront the complexities of reality in a principled yet flexible way. In order to preserve a sense of living a moral life, it has to invoke an absolute code, which covers any eventuality, but which is rigid and potentially brittle. Large reserves of labile aggression are mobilised when breaches of this code by others are discerned, while the individual is unlikely to be able to tolerate any experience that he or she has transgressed this code.

POSTMODERN PROBLEMS

This is a familiar phenomenon in psychoanalytic writings, both in the clinical literature and in social studies such as that of the 'authoritarian personality' (Adorno et al., 1950). Let us now juxtapose it with another piece of contemporary characterology, namely the states of mind suggested by the category 'postmodernism'. Of course we are dealing here with a term that has been highly modish in recent years, with unfortunate consequences for precision, and which even in scholarly contexts has been used with various meanings. It will be used here in a way which emphasises the dissolution of traditional authorities, of stable, massified social blocs and of coherent subjectivities.

The postmodern world, in many descriptions of it, is a world of complex and fluid social differentiations, cultural fragmentation, epistemological and moral relativisms, and un-centred selves. It is a world in which all traditional bases for moral conduct have been discredited or set aside. It is celebrated by some for its allegedly liberatory potential, cautiously welcomed by others, and fiercely regretted by some, for example by those who see it as a state of advanced degeneration resulting from the fundamental social relations of capitalism in which the primacy of exchange value and the cash nexus has corroded all stable human ties and transcendental frameworks.

There are various ways in which psychoanalytic theory might be called upon to describe the postmodern self, and they have been systematically anatomised by Stephen Frosh in *Identity Crisis* (1991). On the whole, in the renderings that Frosh gives of how the Freudian, Kleinian, object-relations and ego-psychology traditions would characterise postmodern states of mind, they are very critical of them, using terms such as narcissism and psychosis to define their essential features. Standing in a somewhat different position, as we would expect, is Lacanian theory, which has on the whole been a source for – rather than a critique of – the postmodern vision, in its polemical assertions of the fictive nature of ego integrity. For the other theories, the unconscious landscapes of postmodern consciousness can be seen as based upon major failures of psychic integration and – in the language of classical psychoanalysis – of superego development. It is useful here to retain the term 'superego', even though it has to some extent been replaced in psychoanalytic language by various descriptions of the world of internal 'object relationships', [3] because it still has important descriptive and connotative functions, and is a point of contact between psychoanalytic discourse and more popular forms of understanding. Many people have got some idea of what it means, and can see its relevance to a discussion of values.

Michael Rustin (1992), rather in contrast to Frosh's review, notes *positive* parallels between some of the premisses of postmodernism as a conceptualisation of cultural change, and the development of a particular tradition in psychoanalysis. The postmodernist focus on phenomenology and its rejection of notions of underlying or overarching truths or structures have affinities, Rustin argues, with the 'post-Kleinian' development in psychoanalysis – the works of Wilfred Bion and Donald Meltzer particularly. This development has moved away from preoccupations with mental structure and mental contents to an arguably more basic concern with how the capacities of the mind to contain experience, to structure itself and to think are formed. To some extent this move is accompanied by an explicit setting aside of theoretical preconception, much in keeping with the relativist tendencies of postmodernist thought, and by a foregrounding of the aesthetic dimension – the latter at least superficially consistent with the postmodernist impulse to demote or deconstruct the ethical.

Rustin concludes, however, that overall this development in psychoanalysis is continuous with the older, humanist traditions of British psychoanalysis, in that it opens up further dimensions along which we can understand the development of selfhood, and adds to our knowledge of the optimum social conditions for enhancing that development. Thus this 'postmodernist' tendency within psychoanalysis can be retrieved within a modernist, humanist project. Fragmentation and moral emptiness are confronted at length within the psychotic or 'borderline' individuals, on work with whom much of this psychoanalysis has focused, but the disintegration is not necessarily installed in a whole vision of society, as it once was in the work of R. D. Laing (1960; 1967).

However, what Rustin calls this 'late Kleinian' perspective is susceptible to other inflections. Frosh, while noting the positive core to Bion's theory in the concepts of reverie and the building up of alpha-function, tends to stress the *diagnostic* resonance of the concepts of beta-elements and bizarre objects, as ways of describing the fragmented psychic world of the post-modern consumer.[4]

Similarly in the collection of essays by Paul Hoggett (1992) there is extensive use of Bion, as well as of Winnicott, Klein and Balint, to develop descriptions of the madness inherent in the everyday. Hoggett's particular concern is with present-day forms of cynicism, which he sees as consisting of thoughtlessness, in a Bionian sense, and attacks on meaning. He links the postmodern disdain for abiding value commitments, at least among a particular political generation, to the failure of the big revolutionary idea. The failure of an object on which one is dependent can lead to attacks not only upon that object but also upon the very idea and possibility of a reliable, good object. So the destruction of meaning is an omnipotent defensive strategy in the context of failed dependency.

To take a further example, Marike Finlay (1989), while not assuming that the postmodern has become culturally dominant, understands it in terms of disintegrative splitting (though Klein rather than Bion is her reference here). She goes on to expound the potential of Winnicottian psychoanalysis to comprehend the evacuation of selfhood which has occurred in the postmodern subject. By offering 'holding' rather than interpretation as a therapeutic strategy, Winnicott engaged with the postmodern refusal of interpretive discourse, and provided a way towards what Finlay suggests is a 'post-postmodern' integration.

So within a predominant mode of psychoanalytic cultural

analysis the two PCs may therefore be seen as defensive reactions against an underlying, 'postmodern' collapse of moral capacity, indeed of the psyche as a whole. To put it in the terms of classical structural theory, the ego and superego no longer provide the firm organisations of experience and impulse on which selfhood depends; a narcissistic, perhaps psychotic, quality permeates the everyday. PC mentalities are strained attempts to occupy the psychic and cultural spaces once more adequately filled by powerful parental imagos, and so to stave off a falling into madness or its normalised form in cynicism.

This kind of psychoanalytic positing of a contemporary malaise predates the rise of theorising about the postmodern. The theory of contemporary culture as narcissistic was advanced by Christopher Lasch in two books published in 1978 and 1984. His work in turn was anticipated in some respects by the outstanding attempts of Philip Rieff in his works of 1959 and 1966 to assess the direction which culture was heading given the success of the Freudian, therapeutic project of freeing individuals from compulsive attachments to traditional authorities. Rieff was the first to use in this context the passage from Yeats' poem to which the title of this chapter alludes ('Things fall apart; the centre cannot hold' – see Rieff, 1966). He was though much more hopeful, in an ironic sort of way, about the prospects for a culture based on the 'analytic attitude' of detachment from the traditions of transcendent meaning.

And before Rieff there stretches in retrospect the work of the Frankfurt School, especially the writings of Erich Fromm (e.g. 1949), and the historical thesis of Horkheimer and Adorno on the decline of the individual (see Horkheimer, 1947). Their very grand historical narrative postulated that during the late capitalist period there has been a radical decay of the major cultural achievement of early, liberal capitalism, namely the moral agency of the individual. Restricted though it was to the bourgeois strata, this liberal self, forged in the heat of the oedipal conflict, was the embodiment of some positive values of self-determination. Freud's structural theory, they argued, subtly described this conflicted but powerful self, and thus provided a model to use in tracing its decline as the combined forces of mass culture and the administrative state left less and less social space for a strong, autonomous ego to establish itself and to ally itself with healthy superego functioning.

We can therefore assemble a quite coherent, interlocking set of psychoanalytical observations on contemporary culture, which posit an underlying dissolution, or at least weakness, of viable, benign superego structures, and which also locate a number of highly moralising discourses as defensive compensations for this state of affairs.[5]

A HUMANIST RECONSTRUCTION?

However, this assumptive framework may be due for a little scrutiny. It is reasonable to ask what evidence there is which can confirm the sense of living in a morally ruined or desolate place, or from which we might have derived the sense of living through, or having a historical perspective on, a general moral collapse. Such a sense animates the kind of theoretical work which has been described. There are of course as many events and situations as ever which are distressing to see or hear about, but it cannot be assumed that these can all be gathered together as expressive of a unified malaise, and as betokening some major, epochal moment of cultural change. Where is the evidence, we should now be asking, for the belief that sufficient numbers of people are so narcissistic, borderline or sub-clinically psychotic in so much of their everyday functioning, and so bereft of inner moral resources, that a language of profound psychopathology and moral crisis is the only one really permitted much space in serious psychocultural critique? While lots of people have got lots of problems, that does not in itself automatically justify the use of heroic diagnostics as the best way of understanding contemporary society.[6]

This line of questioning need not be inspired by the postmodern celebration of the end of unifying narratives; on the contrary it comes here more from a humanist assumption of the primacy of the subject, and a humanist hope that the subject, the self, is a lot more robust than has been assumed.

Such an orientation has been present, implicitly at least, in much of the material of this book. The case studies have been of cultural forms and images, not of individual or collective states of mind, but we expect the latter to be expressed in the former, perhaps even to be shaped by them to some degree. The general argument pursued throughout has been that substantial psychic resources and achievements are embedded in many of the institutions of popular culture. In the areas we have looked at, we do not find overwhelming evidence of psychosocial fragmentation; on the contrary we find (not exclusively, of course, but to an important degree) recurrent tendencies towards integration, reparation and a deeply social commitment.

However, as the discussion in Chapter 2 should have made clear, the case studies have not provided *evidence* in support of this contention, at least not in the social-scientific sense of systematic evidence. Perhaps the next step is to consider what such evidence might be of relevance to the claim that we are in a condition of moral and psychological crisis, and to the counter-claim made here. This takes us into other territories, many and large, beyond the scope of this book, but it may be of interest to indicate something of what they might be. In a sense a major part of the whole discipline of sociology, in both its theoretical and empirical dimensions, has been an attempt to examine the cohesiveness and resilience of social institutions, and changes in social integration, so there is a danger here of reinventing a rather large wheel. Nevertheless some specific areas could be mentioned to give an idea of the sort of interdisciplinary connections which the psychoanalytic study of society needs to make in order to achieve some intellectual integration within current debates about social change and contemporary politics.

EMPIRICAL QUESTIONS

There is firstly the domain of empirical social science, with its attitude surveys and social statistics, some of which are of great relevance to the study of contemporary moralities and of the extent to which some general or absolute principles still command mass respect. Evidence emerging from the annual survey of *British Social Attitudes*, for example, though only begun in the early 1980s, suggests a stable and fairly high level of expressed moral principle on everyday isues such as fiddling expenses, pocketing excess change and overclaiming on insurance (Johnston, 1988). This sort of thing is small beer, perhaps, for those with an eye on the cultural high ground, but then moral fabric does have a fine weave.

Traditionally, and for obvious reasons, crime is taken as a major index of morality, and so there should be much data here that bears on the hypothesis of a (postmodern) moral crisis. There has also been some political consensus of late on the urgency of tackling the rise in certain types of crime, which the figures clearly show. But crime statistics are the basis for another lesson in caution; the data do not speak for themselves, enabling would-be heroes of the Conservative Party Conference to speak for them. The crisis hypothesis requires, in its strongest form, that there has been a significant increase in the proportion of the population who commit crimes, and that this proportion be increasingly distributed across all social groups. Other variants are possible: for instance, that the kinds of crimes committed are becoming more serious, or that criminals – while not increasing in number – are committing more crimes, but these are weaker hypotheses which may also be explicable without recourse to a notion of general moral decline. Criminals might be getting more desperate or persistent, or the police or judicial system less effective in stopping them committing crimes, without there necessarily being a weakening of the moral fabric of society as a whole. On the central question of whether the proportion of people who commit crimes is rising, the data are inevitably unclear, since only one third of all crime is recorded by the police (see Mayhew *et al.*, 1993, p.102), and much less than that attributable to known persons.

We can turn to another key topic in debates about morality, the family, as the crucible of moral feeling. According to the traditional conservative right wing, the family is the scene of a most consequential moral decline, and the critique of Lasch *et al.* of the erosion of parental authority by the state, the welfare professions and the cultures of consumerism have in places converged with that traditional lament. In the conservative view, though, the importance of the 'family' as a social form has been seen as indivisible from some specific moral *content*, including rather narrow codes of sexual conduct and the assertion of a somewhat authoritarian vision of the family. We might nonetheless contend that there are a number of insights and partial truths found in such critique. However we would be hard-pressed to produce any systematic evidence to convince that in this heartland of private morality there has been any overall, substantial dissolution of the readiness and the capacity to live by some basic values.

In the sphere of relationships and parenting, we find that two phenomena have been frequently pointed to by those (not only on the right) wishing to announce the internal collapse of family values: the rising divorce rate and the growing numbers of single parents (who may or may not have once been part of a couple). While the growth in general public awareness of domestic violence and of child abuse may also contribute to the feeling of a gathering crisis of the family, there is no clear evidence that there has been an increase in the actual incidence of either.

Current anxieties about the moral consequences of the spread of single parenthood are consistent with a psychoanalytically informed vision of moral decline. It is not that single parenthood is in itself a sign of moral failure, but rather that it may in some circumstances have the consequence, however unanticipated and unwanted by single parents, of impairing emotional development. Similarly, any psychoanalytic view is going to be concerned about rising rates of divorce and separation, since that implies that the deep pain inevitably experienced by children around the break-up of a parental couple is being experienced by increasing numbers of children. Both social statistics and clinical experience are important sources of data here. However a suspicion of the 'moral panics' associated with polemicists of the right should, in this area, counterbalance any tendency to see things in terms of a massive crisis of values and of social integration. Complex social changes may be taking place in family forms, but change and crisis are not equivalent.

To look at another area of everyday life, and to take a case already discussed in this book, we could look at advertising. This is an area of mundane experience often taken to be at the leading edge of postmodern disintegrative pressures (a critique that has to some degree subsumed the earlier, more moralistic one that advertising has de-moralised the sexual sphere in the last thirty years or so). However, as we saw in Chapter 6, the relations between advertising content and the values and behaviours of the general public are thickly mediated and very complex, and ads cannot be read directly as summaries of the country's morals. And insofar as they can, the picture they give is of a moral universe in which restraint, guilt and responsibility are predominant. Moreover, mainly in response to feminist objections, the sexual content of advertising has changed in the last decade, as well as the portrayals of family life.

Nor does the study of advertising obviously confirm the picture of a descent into postmodern psychosis. There is not yet enough of the right sort of evidence to know what accuracy there may be in such a picture. What we do know is that during the course of this century advertising has progressively detached itself from the actual properties of goods and has dealt more in their symbolic and phantasy meanings. What we cannot say is whether in the kinds of phantasy scenarios represented by advertisements there has been a shift towards more narcissistic or omnipotent themes, or whether advertising is increasingly contributing to a sense of fragmentation in everyday life. There are some impressionistic grounds for thinking that advertising deals today very much in the stuff of oedipal conflicts and depressive anxieties, at least as much as it does in the stuff of more primitive phantasies. We may regret that the provision of symbolic materials for dramatising the work of psychic integration is in the hands of the marketeers, and so is tied to the pursuit of profits and the expansion of markets, but that cannot lead us to prejudge in full the psychic functions which those materials may fulfil for many people.

Another direction in which marketing has changed in the quite recent past is worth mentioning here: that is the way in which it has had to respond to the growth of environmentalist concerns among the consuming public. These are still relatively weak on many fronts, but are regarded by some market researchers as the most significant overall shift in consumer attitudes over the last five years. The history of consumption is in large part the history of how elite or avant-garde practices and sentiments become generalised to a mass market, so we should expect further shifts in this area. Environmentalism is of course psychologically complex (see Chapter 6), but it is hard to dismiss altogether the argument that some new expression of reparative feeling is emerging here.

Speaking of reparation, we might also mention the largely undocumented but great growth in the numbers of people seeking careers in the welfare sector.[7] The appeal of 'counselling' in particular is enormous, and while we might assume it stems in part from students' own needs to be counselled we must also take it at face value as an expression of growing emotional resourcefulness in the culture at large. Nor can the proliferation of counselling practices, trainings and so on be written off as an opportunistic response to the shrinkage of employment prospects in more traditional sectors.

Another more specific and more recent phenomenon relevant to any inquiry into the contemporary moral condition is the growth in charitable activity. Charities are multiplying at a rapid rate (on one estimate, one is being registered every half-hour in Britain – see Jowell *et al.*, 1992), and we have to understand this partly in terms of the withdrawal or contraction of state provision in many areas of welfare. But the scale and success of charitable concerts and television appeals in recent years suggests that involvement in charitable giving (especially to international causes, where it is not so compensatory for neo-liberal policies) may be spreading beyond the middle-class strata to which it has hitherto been largely confined, and may be linked to an advance in altruistic concern. These are speculative suggestions; no argument can be secured here, but the point is that the close study of such phenomena may not support any diagnosis that the present-day world is in the grip of an escalating pathology.

Of course, phenomena such as green shopping, counselling and charitable giving are well known to anyone schooled in leftist social critique as signs that things are getting worse: they are the make-dos of the politically impotent, or they are cynically engineered to provide us with experiences of doing good, but on the ineffectual margins of the world so that the rapacious multinationals can roam free of moral constraint elsewhere, where it really matters. There may indeed be a lot of truth in such cynicism, and it may in some cases be the only appropriate reaction. Whether it is the only one, however, is an empirical question, or rather a whole set of questions about the extent and meanings of changes in consumption patterns and in career choices, the size and use of charitable funds, and so on.

We might ask why questions of this sort have not been raised and explored in much of the broad spectrum of cultural criticism described earlier. In part, this could be attributed to a regrettable tendency in such work to take little interest in systematic empirical studies of social phenomena, usually in the belief that they are likely to be superficial or are so embedded in some alien conceptual framework as to be unusable in the context of psychodynamic study. No doubt the example of some of the early pioneers of socio-psychoanalytic work in the Frankfurt

School is still influential, in their antipathy or ambivalence towards empirical social science.

But we can suggest another reason for why left intellectuals in particular have neglected to consider bodies of evidence which might have checked their preference for diagnostic summaries of contemporary society hanging on some version of the belief that the centre is failing to hold. Why has this *sense* of moral decay become so common a feature of Left social commentary and cultural criticism?

WHY HAVE THEY DONE IT AGAIN?

There has been one aspect of recent British history which a substantial number of people, particularly on the left, have found acutely distressing, namely the Thatcher administration and its aftermath. It may be suggested that the generalised complaint that Britain has become a morally threadbare society stems in part from the despair on the left at the refusal of the electorate to reject Thatcher and her legacy. If people will persistently vote for such shrill self-righteousness and such doctrinaire contemptuousness, trailing such selfish and nationalistic values, then surely – the argument has implicitly run – they must have reached an advanced stage of moral decomposition.

This argument has had a particular appeal to those working in the sectors felt to be most seriously devalued in the climate of the 1980s, which of course are the sectors – the public education, health and welfare services – inhabited by many of the intelligentsia of the left. Faced with sharp declines in the resourcing given and respect paid to one's work, it is tempting to understand this as the expression of a more general neglect of or attack on all goodness, rather than seeing it as part of a more complex and conjunctural process in which a number of moral trajectories can be traced. Many of us gave way to that temptation, and – perhaps in a rather grandiose way – generalised our experience rather too readily into an all-encompassing narrative. The resulting cultural conservatism also became normative in the work of a significant number of media professionals, who for somewhat different reasons (some to do with the defence of public service, some more to do with class and cultural antagonisms) have also felt themselves to be on the defensive in an historic struggle with the forces of darkness embodied in the government.

The result has not been the kind of 'moral panic' traditionally associated with the patriotically correct right, nor its left equivalent in the kind of moralistic campaign typical of 'political correctness'. These depend, as we have noted, on the presence of strong persecuted and persecutory feelings, which are not so intense among the majority of this broad left-liberal political constituency. The result instead tends to remain at the level of a rather self-righteous gloom, a despair at the way things have gone. This has slotted into an unfortunate inter-relationship with the even more self-righteous tendency of some neo-liberal polemicists to castigate their opponents (the 'moaning minnies') for their alleged denigration of the British nation. The result is a sterile, repetitive interchange between one group of people puffing out their chests, and another group beating their breasts. This is an example of a classic intergroup dynamic, each complaining party needing the other to contain some part of itself and thus justify the argument. The Thatcherites and some of their opponents needed each other to represent disowned parts of themselves. This seems to have been illustrative of the sado-masochistic sort of relationship characteristic of the Thatcher administration's dealings with various others, and which she in particular enjoyed in a number of contexts.

Moreover, Thatcher was for some people a mere insult added to the more fundamental injury of the 1970s, which lay in the failure of the revolutionary impulse. Capitalism, having won the showdown of 1968, went on to rub the faces of the radical left in their defeat by allowing the forces of neo-liberalism to sweep to power in a number of countries. The complicity of electorates in this development is arguably the main reason why so many on the left drew the conclusion that we are living in a time of profound moral malaise.

To some extent the sense of malaise is a feature of the intellectual classes rather than of the self-conscious left. Intellectuals are almost by definition one of the most disenchanted groups in any society. This in a sense is what they are here for, to articulate and carry a disproportionate share of the collective burden of mourning and disappointment. But, by analogy with a 'late Kleinian' model of psychotherapeutic work, what they should be doing with this feeling of disenchantment is to contain and de-toxify it, and return it to the wider culture in forms that can be accepted and used creatively. What should not happen, on this model, is that the intellectual class *amplifies* the depression split off and projected into them by the triumphant neo-liberal nationalists. Perhaps psychoanalytic intellectuals are more vulnerable to getting caught up in this kind of projection because of their spontaneous orientation to the pathological, given the clinical basis of psychoanalytic theory. However this is one of a number of the difficulties facing psychoanalytic intellectuals who want to position themselves in relation to the wider culture (see Chapter 9).

Whatever its sources, there is in the belief in cultural collapse an unsupportable monism at work, an unjustified inference from a particular to the general. Moral capacity is not a single psychosocial entity, the exercise of which must yield a uniform result across all the different spheres of life. There are no logical, psychological or social reasons why people may not display different kinds and degrees of moral sensibility in different contexts. Indeed it is commonplace to observe how this can be the case – how the mafia boss may be nice to children, or the money market speculator be a major philanthropist. We are not referring here to examples of hypocrisy, to ego-dystonic moral cleavages in the lives of some individuals, but rather to the usual complexity of human action. Psychoanalysis emphatically underscores this point, in the attention it pays to the intricacy of object relations in the internal world, and the endless variety of ways in which internal objects can find representation in the external world.

The theory of the superego, specifically, has recognised the multiple origins of this agency, the ways in which a variety of pre-oedipal components are brought together and then subsequently added to or 'refined' by a range of social influences. That these diverse components are seen as being welded together in the action of a higher principle (whether through the resolution of the oedipus complex or in the consolidation of the depressive organisation) does not require us to think of the resulting agency as a simple monolith. The superego coalesces around a range of identifications made for different reasons with different kinds of objects. Moral regulation today is not monolithic, and there are no psychological reasons to suggest that it should be, unless we wish to re-install the kind of tyrannical superego embodied in the Protestant doctrines of the early modern period.

So, filled though one may be with sorrow and anger at the style and a good deal of the substance of government in recent years, and at the support apparently given to it, we cannot deduce from the regrettable condition of the British polity that the British people in some overall way have entered a period of deep moral impoverishment. Something is certainly wrong, psychoculturally, with a society which could award itself such government four times over, but the problem is both more limited and more complex than is allowed by the almost-despairing diagnostics of the left.

In that style of social theorising, we can probably see the inspiration of the Laingian inversion of madness and normality. However little explicit reference is made in such work to Laing, it is plausible to suggest that the extraordinary impact of his writing upon many people in the 1960s accounts in part for the strength of this belief today in the brooding madness beneath the surface of the mundane. It has since then been widely understood that the task of psychoanalytic cultural criticism is to specify the particular forms of madness inscribed in normality, and to give us some clues as to the origins and supports of such madness in socio-economic change and its impact upon inner life. And since Klein, we have had before us a most forceful expression of the view that madness and the moral dimension are as one, that madness and badness tap common developmental roots.

As Hoggett (1992) points out, this approach has a built-in one-dimensionality when applied unchecked to society. The complexity of a culture is likely to get lost in such a diagnostic discourse, even where there are alternative diagnoses available and where many of them bring a unique perspicacity and empathic richness to their subject. Among many examples that could come to mind, Adorno's (1951) essay on fascist propaganda is powerfully illuminating in some of its observations, however hopelessly totalising or elitist its author's overall world view may now seem.

But it is not clear that Hoggett's alternative to this mode is likely to be much different. He remarks that in psychoanalytic theory we are conceived of as continually moving between different states of mind – Bion's Ps<>D, the continual movement in psychic life between primitive paranoid-schizoid states and more integrated, realistic depressive ones. In our studies of culture and society we should therefore expect to find oscillations between more and less mature and integrated modes. The cultural analyst however appears to be free to acknowledge this reminder but to continue to focus heavily on the pathological, and to convey that it is the Ps states which are predominant in the culture at large.

One reason for trying to extricate us from an unthinking commitment to big diagnostics lies in the kind of rhetorical orientations that tend to flow from such commitment, whether or not the diagnoses may be to some degree accurate. It is not on the whole favourable to making an effective intervention in debates in the public sphere to have as a major premiss that, to put it crudely, we are living in a madhouse. People may become defensive, and it may be hard to see what sorts of remedial action may be most effectively taken. The failure of psychoanalytic thinking to have much effect on the peace movement, even at the height of cold war paranoia, is one example of the difficulties faced by diagnostic discourse in translating itself into political effectivity. We might also cite the arrogance and paranoia embedded in the ideas that all men hate women or that all whites are racist as instances of very unhelpful (and untrue) pathologising. Pockets of primitive ambivalence towards women, and at least residual constellations of splitting around race would have to be admitted to by any male or white person, and some are in the grip of such forms of ugliness. But to privilege and then universalise such judgments and pronounce us all as sick at heart is the most crass of dogmatisms, and Hughes *et al.* rightly pour scorn on these positions. Nor may more subtle accounts of cultural dis-ease make much impact on those who sense that the psychic pattern of everyday life is not as crazed as these theories would have it.

DEMOCRACIES OF FEELING

Alongside the many insights that psychoanalysis can bring about the anxieties and defences that are layered into everyday experience, we should also draw from it a sense of the resilience of moral capacity. One review of psychoanalytic theories of the superego (Rothstein, 1983) takes its cue from an early formulation of Freud's which locates the origin of moral capacities in the fact of infantile helplessness. Rothstein comments that 'The original function of ... [the] superego is to provide the developing child with an inner sense of the parents' presence' (p. 51).

This simple, moving idea, consistent with a range of different psychoanalytic perspectives, suggests a benign and transhistorical depth to the superego, a capacity for the spontaneous development of a moral sense that social change of any kind may modulate but not radically impair across a whole culture. As Freud himself put it in one of his later works:

> If anyone were inclined to put forward the paradoxical proposition that the normal man is not only far more immoral than he believes but also far more moral than he knows, psychoanalysis, on whose findings the first half of the assertion rests, would have no objection to raise against the second half (Freud, 1923, p. 52).

The kind of use to which Freud and the post-Freudians have been put in this book goes against the grain of most recent psychoanalytic theorising about culture. Much of this, as I have described, has tended towards the diagnostic mode; the aim has been to identify the prevalent forms of pathology, to reveal the dis-ease in contemporary culture. Here the aim has been to develop and illustrate a different kind of approach, one which emphasises the containing and integrating functions of some key institutions of popular culture. These constitute democracies of feeling; the experiences they provide utilise aesthetic codes which are not the product of any exclusive educational or cultural socialisation but which are part of a common cultural weal.

The case studies in Part II have argued, against all forms of elitism, that there is emotional depth and authenticity in the life of these institutions. Further case studies (e.g. of the moral qualities of television 'soap operas', on which there already is a substantial literature, or of the tabloid press, or of popular radio) would be necessary (both in the 'critical' mode illustrated here, and in a more research-based mode) to assess the extent to which these qualities are common to other major forms of mass cultural consumption.

Yet if the analyses offered here are basically sound, even if only for the particular examples they deal with, and however much they need to be qualified and complemented by more negative observations, then they register a dimension of human experience which must be addressed by social and cultural theory. Emotional involvement in the sorts of cultural practice which have been discussed (whether as participant or audience, producer or consumer) offers the containment of intense libidinality by good, accepted parental objects. It posits the person as the universal subject of a shared authority, and makes social membership intensely gratifying. At the core of the book's analyses has been the idea that the pleasures of popular culture are at their strongest and best when they confirm us in our sense of belonging to an inclusive social order. Despite the constraint and disappointment necessarily involved in this, the reconciliation with authority which it brings is vital for the containment of feelings about loss, destructiveness and death with which we are continually struggling.

It has been suggested in this chapter that we may have been mistaking the un-ease in culture for dis-ease, the intrinsic tensions for contingent ills. Perhaps we should be more specific and more concrete about what troubles us; we might then find we are dealing with forms of ordinary unhappiness rather than neurotic misery, let alone the psychotic crumbling of the self. Any reasonably complex account of modern society can recognise that there is no 'centre' as such – we do not need the category of the postmodern to help us make that observation – but poetically speaking it is probably more true to say that the centre is holding than that things are falling apart.

NOTES

1: THE DEPTHS OF THE ORDINARY

1. These particular examples might not seem to be the best ones to illustrate particularity. The chat show and counselling could both be described as institutionalised forms of conversation, or of encounters with 'personalities', and therefore both be seen as products of an age in which the revelation of the inner person through specific procedures of conversation is a much-demanded experience. The hypermarket and the car boot sale could be seen as complementary, with the latter meeting some need for contingent, face-to-face, individualised and non-practical forms of exchange and shopping, needs not met in the regulated, impersonal, massified and highly practical visits to the hypermarket. While recognising the interest and possible value of such connection-making, however, we need not overlook the obvious specificities of all of these phenomena, each of which may require a number of other factors to be considered if it is to be adequately understood.

2. Of course a significant number of people are excluded by absolute poverty from some of the experiences to be discussed. But for the domiciled majority with some degree of disposable income, the opportunity to consume these experiences is generally available.

3. The ancient recognition of the impossibility of full satisfaction of human desire has recently been re-emphasised by followers of the Lacanian psychoanalytic school. The reading of Freud which informs the present work differs from the Lacanian in some important respects, but certainly shares a stress on the inevitability of disappointment. See my book *Images of Freud*, for a summary of the basic understanding of psychoanalysis, and of what it says about human nature, which underlies the approach taken here to popular culture. Parts of that book, however, are

inflected by the antipathy to mass culture and popular consumption from which I have in this present work been trying to disengage.

4. This would not be true of the Lacanian literature on popular culture, which has concentrated on some cinema and literary forms, and which has been more ambivalent towards the popular. See, e.g., Zizek, 1991.

2:   WHAT IS THE PSYCHOANALYTIC STUDY OF CULTURE?

1. An earlier draft of this chapter was given as a talk on research methods in psychoanalytic studies to the postgraduate seminar at the Centre for Psychoanalytic Studies, University of Kent, in February 1993.

2. This conceptual shift is closely linked to another in psychoanalysis, one which has overlain the theorisations of the influence in the unconscious of early familial relationships with a stress on the ubiquity and the impact of psychotic anxieties and of mental processes at a level 'beneath' the formation of stable images of others. Generally speaking, the orientation of this book is more towards the former outlook, in a mixture of Freudian, Kleinian and object-relational terms; the later one is discussed briefly in Chapter 10.

3. I have dealt elsewhere (1989a, pp. 26–30) with the fallacious argument that only clinicians are entitled to use psychoanalytic concepts in the study of non-clinical phenomena.

4. There are also Adorno's (1967) strictures about the tendencies to parasitism and apologetics in the role of the cultural critic, and – from a very different direction – the antipathy towards 'intellectualising' about everyday life. However, neither Adorno nor the 'no nonsense' brigade start with the assumption that popular culture contains much of depth and value.

5. There is a still small but growing amount of work of this sort. The psychoanalyst Isabel Menzies-Lyth has produced

some of the classic examples of such work, both in the fields of health and welfare provision and in studies of everyday culture – see Chapters 5 and 6. For a more recent example of the former see Cooper (1992); in the latter category, some work in progress at the University of East London on advertising and cultural change will draw heavily upon psychoanalytic understanding.

3:   THE GLORY OF THE GAME

1. This chapter has grown out of a paper on 'The passion for football', given at a conference on 'Psychoanalysis and Popular Culture' held at the Royal College of Art, London, in March 1991, and at a symposium on 'Psychoanalysis and Popular Culture' at the Centre for Psychoanalytic Studies, University of Kent, in April 1991.

2. In this respect the 1863 meeting was just one stage in a long process which began in the mid-nineteenth century (and arguably still continues), a process involving not only the development of football but an increasing regulation and codification of many areas of life – in all forms of mass entertainment, in the growth of welfare services, in changes in work organisation, and in government. This process has been the subject of much research and debate in recent years, work which will only be touched upon here though much of it is relevant to a rounded understanding of the social meaning of something like football. From different viewpoints, this process involves an imposition of bourgeois rationality or administrative logic on the flux of life, or laying the foundations of the civil and moral order of modern society, or a middle-class mission to improve the workers, or the creation of new forms of subjectivity in the emergent 'mass society'. I will be suggesting that in the case of football at least, whatever sociological descriptions fit, it was primarily a creative and positive process, a 'civilising' of the increasingly important leisure sphere.

3. Some of these 'rituals' seem short-lived. In the late 1980s players going onto the field as substitutes during matches in Britain were given affectionate pats with a cupped hand on the lower bottom by the manager or coach on the touch-

line. This practice seems to have faded out as quickly and with as little explanation as it began.

4. Murphy *et al.* (1989) also show that while disorder at British football matches may have increased in the last twenty years, the most striking change has been in the attitudes towards it adopted in the media, which have brought it to public attention in a sometimes alarmist way, and arguably amplified it.

4:   THE BODY OF THE NATION

1. This chapter is based on a paper on 'Ethnicity and the Countryside', given at the 1992 'Psychoanalysis and the Public Sphere' Conference, University of East London, in October 1992, and at a seminar of the New Ethnicities Research Group at the University of East London, in March 1993.

2. The discussion presented here must admit to many gaps and rough edges, and begs a lot of questions. What, for example, of the category of the 'non-white'? It may reflect the phantasied whiteness of the landscape to use such a negative category, but it certainly won't do in any analytical sense, since all kinds of identities and phantasies are brought to the edge of the countryside by different kinds of 'non-white' people.

3. It is not unusual for manual workers to refer to large stones and other obstacles to their task with the masculine pronoun.

4. This knowledge may not obtain elsewhere. As Romany-shyn and Whalen (1987) describe, the American attitude towards the countryside – more in keeping with the Puritan world-view – has been coloured more by a need to dominate and transform it. In Britain, notwithstanding the Romantic tradition of reacting against the neatness and order of the agricultural landscape, and the accompanying aesthetic preference for mountain, rock and untamed nature (Thomas, 1983, pp. 258–69), the desired countryside has largely been domesticated.

5. This still leaves the argument in an unsatisfactory condition. I am aware that in referring to contagious magic I am casting around for a way of making theoretical sense of the observations which provided this chapter's starting point.

6. For example, my own experience of the beauty of the Cornish coastal path is shadowed by the thought of the hellish tin mines beneath and of miners walking to work in them. I may be unusually preoccupied with such thoughts, coming from a family where a majority of the men who have lived this century have worked underground, but there are many such families in Britain.

7. The potential force of this convention is illustrated by the story of the two IRA terrorists who were reconnoitring the countryside around the house of a British Cabinet minister. They failed to say hello to a local walker, who alerted the police and so led to their arrest.

5: THE GREAT CAR SOCIETY

1. Part of this chapter is based on a paper on 'Technophilia and Technophobia', given at a conference on 'Ecological Madness: Psychoanalysis and our Ecological Dilemmas', organised by the Freud Museum and held at Sutton House, London, on 5 December 1992, and subsequently published in the *British Journal of Psychotherapy* 10(2), 1993. It also includes some material from articles published in *Free Associations* 1989, the *Sunday Correspondent* 1989, and the *Guardian*, 1990. Readers may discern a more polemical note in this chapter than elsewhere, because of the direct relevance of the issues explored here to some charged areas of contemporary debate.

2. The theme of hope has been especially clearly shown in TV advertising campaigns for Rover and Vauxhall, using minidramas about weddings and births.

3. For a discussion of some examples of technophobia in this sphere see Richards, 1985a.

6:    GOODS AND GOOD OBJECTS

1. This chapter derives from a paper on 'Psychoanalysis, Consumption and Market Research' given as part of a Symposium on Psychoanalysis and Consumption at the 1991 'Psychoanalysis and the Public Sphere' Conference, University of East London, in November 1991.

2. See, for example, Schudson, 1993; Wernick, 1991; Nava and Nava, 1991.

3. This possibility was suggested to me by Bob Young.

7:    MUSIC FOR ALL THE FAMILY

1. The last part of this chapter is based on an article that appeared in *Free Associations* in 1987.

2. For a wonderful example, dig out your – or your parents' – Fleetwood Mac *Rumours* LP.

8:    PAIN IN THE SUBURBS

1. This chapter is based on a paper on 'Popular music and the containment of psychic pain', given at the 1990 'Psychoanalysis and the Public Sphere' Conference, University of East London, in October 1990.

2. One can get some sense of this from the information in Ray Coleman's (1985) biography.

3. Incidentally, this passionate faithfulness to the blues contrasts notably with another aspect of his life, especially during his early period of fervent adoration of the blues, and that is the extraordinary variability in his appearance. Comparing photos of Clapton in the 1960s and 1970s one would not know that one were looking at the same person unless one read the captions. His co-members of the Yardbirds comment how Eric was always inscrutably changing, anticipating every fashion by being at odds with the prevailing one. He used

fashion as a serial disguise, swirling around a constant musical identity. Notably, since the mid-1980s, Clapton is – while still a sharp stylist – now recognisable from one photograph to another.

4. Willeford (1985), in an interesting essay on blues by a Jungian analyst, makes a similar distinction between 'the blues as having the blues and the blues as musical poetry', or between blues as experiential 'terrain' and as a distancing 'map' of that territory.

5. So, of course, is the leading guitar-smasher Pete Townshend, a good friend of Clapton. Although a very important figure in the history of pop, Townshend's musical work is not usually seen as having the depth or virtuosity of Clapton's and Hendrix's; there was perhaps less at stake for him in his relationship with his guitar.

6. At the conference at which I presented an earlier version of this chapter, several people remarked that for them the image of 'holding on' was a sexual one. It is clearly the case in some songs (and particularly in the 'funk' tradition which is one indirect descendant of blues) that it is a cry to delay climax. Overall though my argument here is for the primacy in blues of loss, and the kind of desire with which it is associated, over the more performative and genital aspects.

7. In the work of many blues musicians we find re-enactments of Robert Johnson's nightmare of 'a hellhound on my trail'.

8. What precise theorisation is most appropriate for thinking about this resource is a matter for debate amongst the various positions available within contemporary psychoanalysis. The tendency here has been to think of it in classical Kleinian terms as an experience of repair and recovery. The 'post-Kleinian' view would suggest that some pristine experience of the sublime could be involved.

9:   WHAT DO THE PEOPLE WANT?

1. I tried to characterise and explain some of this hostility in *Images of Freud* (1989a) – see Chapter 1, Note 3. Its

consequences, in the limited impact of psychoanalytic ideas, were briefly discussed earlier in the present book, at the beginning of Chapter 6.

2. Cioffi proposed this argument in the mid-1970s, but unfortunately he has not published the work he has done on this issue (personal communication, March 1994).

10:   THE CENTRE IS PROBABLY HOLDING

1. Some of the material in this chapter was presented in a paper on 'The Postmodern Superego' at the 1993 'Psycho-analysis and the Public Sphere' Conference, University of East London, in November 1993.

2. For example Melanie Phillips again, and – making his third appearance in this book – her *Observer* colleague Simon Hoggart, who has long been an angrily amused chronicler of 'Political Correctness'.

3. The concept of an 'object' has been used in a number of places, hopefully in contexts that have given it meaning for those readers unfamiliar with it. Since it denotes a basic entity of mental life it is fundamental to the kind of post-Freudian thinking which informs much of this book. The concept is bound up with that of the 'inner world'. As individual subjects we are in relationship to the world of external reality and the 'objects' in it (the term is used technically, as the complement of 'subject'; it therefore includes other people, who are in fact the most important kind of 'object'). But in addition we live in a world of internal reality, of unconscious phantasy, in which we feel ourselves to contain a host of 'objects' (good, bad and indifferent) in different kinds of relationships with each other and with our inner representations of ourselves.

4. In Bion's theory of thinking there are some powerful images of fragmentation: beta elements are 'undigested' frag-ments of experience to which the individual has failed to give meaning via the creative 'alpha-function'. Bizarre objects are features of schizophrenic experience, when the subject's own capacities to perceive have – because of the anxiety they

generate in a mind unable to tolerate reality – been commi-
nuted and projected into external objects. These are then felt
to have bizarre and threatening qualities, further reducing the
subject's capacity to process experience. Reverie is the state
of mind required of the baby's mother such that she can
tolerate the terrifying feelings which the baby will project into
her, and thus provide the baby with a model of how
experience can be contained and thought about, rather than
overwhelming the ego. It is therefore the source of the
developing infant's capacity for alpha-function (see Bion,
1967). These concepts are now seen by some psychoanalysts
as central to the contemporary psychoanalytic paradigm. A
'late Kleinian' approach has been applied in some reflections
on 'high' culture (e.g. Waddell and Williams, 1991, who seek
to locate a vital source of psychoanalysis itself in the literary
tradition), but has not so far been taken up in relation to the
sorts of topic discussed in this book.

5. This kind of understanding loosely informed the collection
of papers called *Crises of the Self* and which I edited in 1989,
which were drawn from the first 'Psychoanalysis and the
Public Sphere' conferences. It included contributions by Frosh
and Hoggett among a number of studies of the 'postmodern'
psyche.

6. In the context of the conference at which an earlier version
of part of this chapter was presented, these questions were
posed with some apprehension, as if they were atheistic
mutterings during a church service. The assumption under
scrutiny has been implicitly written in to much of what has
happened at those conferences and in much related work. For
some writers (including, for a considerable time, the present
author) the elucidation of our collective immorality or mad
amorality is the main business of the whole project of
psychoanalytic studies.

7. Experience at the University of East London, for example,
is of thousands of people drawn towards courses in social
sciences because they are seen as providing the academic
grounding for working in the welfare sector. Demand for this
sort of pre-vocational course did not seem to decline even
when the social standing of the welfare professions became
much less assured in the 1980s.

REFERENCES

Adorno, T. *et al.* (1950) *The Authoritarian Personality*. New York: Harper & Row.
—— (1951) 'Freudian theory and the pattern of fascist propaganda', in A. Arato and E. Gebhardt, eds., *The Essential Frankfurt School Reader*, Oxford: Blackwell, 1978, pp. 118–37.
—— (1967) 'Cultural criticism and society', in *Prisms*, trans. S. and S. Weber, 17–34. Cambridge, Mass.: MIT Press, 1983.

Barrett, M. and Mcintosh, M. (1982) 'Narcissism and the family: a critique of Lasch', *New Left Review* 135, pp. 35–8.
Bertaux, D., ed. (1981) *Biography and Society*, Beverly Hills: Sage.
Bettelheim, B. (1990) *Recollections and Reflections*. London: Thames and Hudson.
Bion, W. (1967) *Second Thoughts*. London: Heinemann.
Blanchflower, D. (1958) 'Will Cinderella get caught out?' *Observer*, 7 June 1958.
Booker, C. (1969) *The Neophiliacs*. London: Collins.
Brooks, P. (1987) 'The idea of a psychoanalytic literary criticism', in S. Rimmon–Kenan, ed., *Discourse in Psychoanalysis and Literature*, London: Methuen, pp. 1–18.
Burnham, J. (1979) 'From avant–garde to specialism: psychoanalysis in America', *Journal of the History of the Behavioral Sciences*. 15, pp. 128–34.

Campbell, C. (1987) *The Romantic Ethic and the Spirit of Modern Consumerism*. Oxford: Blackwell.
Carey, J. (1992) *The Intellectuals and the Masses: Pride and Prejudice among the Literary Intelligentsia 1880–1939*. London: Faber & Faber.
Chasseguet–Smirgel, J. (1985) *The Ego Ideal: A Psychoanalytic Essay on the Malady of the Ideal*. London: Free Association Books.

— (1986) *Sexuality and Mind: The Role of the Father and the Mother in the Psyche*. New York: New York University Press.

Cioffi, F., ed. (1973) *Freud*. London: Macmillan.

Coleman, R. (1985) *Survivor: The Authorized Biography of Eric Clapton*. London: Futura, 1986.

Cooper, A. (1992) 'Anxiety and child protection in two national systems', *Journal of Social Work Practice* 6(2), pp. 117–28.

Culf, A. (1994) 'Benetton defends shock ad', *Guardian*, 16 February 1994.

Cunliffe, J. and Berridge, C. (1987) *My Postman Pat Storytime Book*. London: Treasure.

Dahmer, H. (1993) 'Psychoanalytic social research', *Free Associations* 28, pp. 490–9.

Denzin, N. (1989) *Interpretive Biography*. London: Sage.

Dervin, D. (1985) 'The psychoanalysis of sport' in J. Prager and M. Rustin, eds., *Psychoanalytic Sociology* Vol. 2. Aldershot: Elgar, 1993, pp. 160–82.

Deutsch, H. (1926) 'A contribution to the psychology of sport', *International Journal Psycho–Analysis* 7, pp. 223–37.

Dichter, E. (1960) *The Strategy of Desire*. London: Boardman.

— (1964) *Handbook of Consumer Motivation*. New York: McGraw–Hill.

Dundy, E. (1985) *Elvis and Gladys: The Genesis of the King*. London: Weidenfeld & Nicholson.

Dunning, E., (1971) 'The development of modern football', in E. Dunning, ed., *The Sociology of Sport*, London: Cass, pp. 133–51.

Easlea, B. (1983) *Fathering the Unthinkable*. London: Pluto.

Elias, N. (1939) *The Civilising Process. Vol. 1: The History of Manners*. Oxford: Blackwell, 1978.

— (1939) *The Civilising Process. Vol. 2: State Formation and Civilisation*. Oxford: Blackwell, 1982.

Elias, N. and Dunning, E. (1971) 'Folk football in medieval and early modern Britain', in E. Dunning, ed., *The Sociology of Sport*, London: Cass, pp. 117–32.

Figlio, K. (1989) 'Unconscious aspects of health and the public sphere', in B. Richards, ed., 1989b, pp. 85–99.

— (1993) 'Commentary on "The mirror and the hammer".' *Free Associations* 28, pp. 594–603.

Finlay, M. (1989) 'Post–modernizing psychoanalysis/Psycho-analyzing post–modernism', *Free Associations* 16, pp. 43–80.

Foucault, M. (1975) *Discipline and Punish: The Birth of the Prison.* Harmondsworth: Penguin, 1979.

Frazer, J. G. (1911) *The Golden Bough: Part 1. The Magic Art and the Evolution of Kings. Vol. 1.* London: Macmillan.

Freud, S. (1911) 'Formulations on the Two Principles of Mental Functioning', in *The Standard Edition of the Complete Psychological Works of Sigmund Freud* (hereafter '*SE*'), Vol. XII, London: Hogarth, pp. 213–26.

—— (1913) 'Totem and Taboo', *SE* Vol. XIII, pp. 1–161.

—— (1921) 'Group Psychology and the Analysis of the Ego', *SE* Vol. XVIII, pp. 69–143.

—— (1923) 'The Ego and the Id', *SE* Vol. XIX, pp. 12–66.

—— (1926) 'Inhibitions, Symptoms and Anxiety', *SE* Vol. XX, pp. 87–172.

Frith, S. and Horne, H. (1987) *Art Into Pop.* London: Methuen.

Fromm, E. (1949) *Man for Himself: An Inquiry into the Psychology of Ethics.* London: Ark.

Frontori, L., Paris, A. and Ventura, I. (1989) 'Association technique and jingle analysis', *Proceedings of the ESOMAR Congress,* Stockholm 1989, pp. 443–60.

Frosh, S. (1991) *Identity Crisis: Modernity, Psychoanalysis and the Self.* Basingstoke: Macmillan.

Hale, N., Jr. (1971) *Freud and the Americans.* Oxford: Oxford University Press.

Hall, S. and Jefferson, T., eds (1976) *Resistance Through Rituals.* London: Hutchinson.

Hering, C. (1994) 'The problem of the Alien: emotional mastery or emotional fascism in contemporary film production'. *Free Associations* 31, 391–407.

Hill, D. (1989) *Out of his Skin: The John Barnes Phenomenon.* London: Faber.

Hinshelwood, R. (1989) *A Dictionary of Kleinian Thought.* London: Free Association Books.

—— (1993) 'The countryside', *British Journal of Psychotherapy* 10(2), pp. 202–210.

Hoggart, S. (1990) 'In praise of pre–art pop', *Observer Magazine* 4 March 1990, p. 3.

Hoggett, P. (1992) *Partisans in an Uncertain World: The Psychoanalysis of Engagement.* London: Free Association Books.

Horkheimer, M. (1947) *Eclipse of Reason.* New York: Seabury, 1974.

Hornby, N. (1992) *Fever Pitch*. London: Gollancz.

Hoskins, W. (1955) *The Making of the English Landscape*. Harmondsworth: Penguin, 1970.

Hughes, R. (1993) *Culture of Complaint: The Fraying of America*. New York: Oxford University Press.

Johnston, M. (1988) 'The price of honesty', in Jowell, R., Witherspoon, S., and Brook, L., eds. *British Social Attitudes: The Fifth Report*, Aldershot: Gower, pp. 1–15.

Jowell, R., *et al.*, eds (1992) *British Social Attitudes: The Ninth Report*. Aldershot: Gower.

Laing, R. D. (1960) *The Divided Self*. Harmondsworth: Penguin, 1965.

— (1967) *The Politics of Experience*. Harmondsworth: Penguin.

Lasch, C. (1978) *The Culture of Narcissism*. New York: Norton.

— (1984) *The Minimal Self*. New York: Norton.

Lazer, W. (1973) 'Marketing research: past accomplishments and potential future developments', *Journal of the Market Research Society* 16(3), pp. 183–202.

Leiss, W., Kline, S. and Jhally, S. (1990) *Social Communication in Advertising* (2nd edn). London: Routledge.

Lunt, P. and Livingstone, S. (1992) *Mass Consumption and Personal Identity*. Buckingham: Open University Press.

MacCabe, C., ed. (1986) *High Theory/Low Culture*. Manchester: Manchester University Press.

Marsh, D. (1987) *Glory Days. A Biography of Bruce Springsteen*. London: Sidgwick and Jackson.

Mason, T. (1981) *Association Football and English Society 1863–1915*. Brighton: Harvester.

— (1989) 'Football', in T. Mason, ed., *Sport in Britain: A Social History*, Cambridge: Cambridge University Press, pp. 146–86.

Mayhew, P., et al.. (1993) *The 1992 British Crime Survey*. London: HMSO.

Menzies-Lyth, I. (1989) 'The driver's dilemma', in *The Dynamics of the Social*, London: Free Association Books, pp. 124–41.

Mitchell, J. (1974) *Psychoanalysis and Feminism*. Harmondsworth: Penguin.

Murphy, P., Williams, J. and Dunning, E. (1990) *Football on Trial*. London: Routledge.

Nava, M. and Nava, O. (1991) 'Discriminating or duped? Young people as consumers of advertising art', *Magazine of Cultural Studies* 1, pp. 15–21.

Nowell–Smith, G. (1987) 'Popular culture', *New Formations* 2, pp. 79–90.

Pearson, G. (1983) *Hooligan. A History of Respectable Fears.* London: Macmillan.

Pickford, R. (1940) 'The psychology of the history and organisation of association football', *British Journal of Psychology* 31, pp. 80–93.

Pidgeon, J. (1985) *Eric Clapton. A Biography.* London: Vermilion.

Richards, B. (1985a) 'Reproductive technology and Left morality', *New Statesman* 2833, pp. 23–5.

—— (1985b) 'The politics of the self' *Free Associations* 3, pp. 43–64.

—— (1987) 'Bruce Springsteen and the crisis of masculinity', *Free Associations* 9, pp. 91–4.

—— (1989a) *Images of Freud: Cultural Responses to Psychoanalysis.* London: Dent.

——, ed. (1989b) *Crises of the Self.* London: Free Association Books.

—— (1993) 'Technophobia and technophilia', *British Journal of Psychotherapy* 10 (2), pp. 188–95.

—— (1994) 'The cultural predicaments of psychoanalysis', *Free Associations* 32, pp. 549–69.

Rieff, P. (1959) *Freud: The Mind of the Moralist.* London: Gollancz.

—— (1966) *The Triumph of the Therapeutic.* Chicago: University of Chicago Press, 1987.

Ritzer, G. (1992) *The Macdonaldization of Society.* London: Sage.

Romanyshyn, R. and Whalen, B. (1987) 'Depression and the American dream: the struggle with home', in D. Levin, ed., *Pathologies of the Modern Self.* New York: New York University Press, pp. 198–220.

Rosenthal, G. (1990) 'The structure and "gestalt" of autobiography and its methodological consequences', *Proceedings of the XIIth World Congress of Sociology*, Madrid.

Rothstein, A. (1983) *The Structural Hypothesis: An Evolutionary Perspective.* New York: International Universities Press.

Rustin, M. (1992) *The Good Society and the Inner World*. London: Verso.
Rustin, M. and Rustin, M. (1987) *Narratives of Love and Loss*. London: Verso.

Samuels, A. (1993) *The Political Psyche*. London: Routledge.
Schudson, M. (1986) *Advertising: The Uneasy Persuasion*. London: Routledge, 1993.
Searles, H. (1960) *The Nonhuman Environment in Normal Development and in Schizophrenia*. New York: International Universities Press.
Sekoff, J. (1989) 'Amnesia, romance and the mind–doctor film' in B. Richards, ed., 1989b, pp. 147–80.
Shaw, J. (1994) 'Transference and Counter-transference in the Mass Observation Archive', in *Human Relations*, forthcoming.
Stokes, A. (1956) 'Psychoanalytic reflections on the development of ball games, particularly cricket', *International Journal of Psycho–Analysis* 37, pp. 185–92.
Suarez–Orozco, M. (1993) 'A psychoanalytic study of Argentine soccer', in Boyer, L., Boyer, R. and Sonnenberg, S., eds, *The Psychoanalytic Study of Society Vol. 18: Essays in honour of Alan Dundes*. Hillsdale, N.J.: The Analytic Press.

Thomas, K. (1983) *Man and the Natural World*. Harmondsworth: Penguin, 1984.
Turner, S. (1976) *Conversations with Eric Clapton*. London: Abacus.

Veblen, T. (1899) *The Theory of the Leisure Class*. New York: Viking, 1948.

Walsh, M. (1990) 'Motor vehicles and the environment: a research agenda'. Paper presented at international conference on the Automotive Industry and the Environment, Geneva, November 1990.
Wernick, A. (1991) *Promotional Culture*. London: Sage.
Willeford, W. (1985) 'Abandonment, wish and hope in the blues'. *Chiron* 1985, pp. 173–201.
Williams, H. (1991) *Autogeddon*. London: Cape.
Williams, M.H. and Waddell, M. (1991) *The Chamber of Maiden Thought: Literary Origins of the Psychoanalytic Model of the Mind*. London: Routledge.

Williams, R. (1983) *Keywords* (2nd edn). London: Fontana.

Williamson, J. (1990) 'Taking Stock'. *Guardian* 8 February 1990.

Willis, P. (1990) *Common Culture*. Milton Keynes: Open University Press.

Wilson, E. (1985) *Adorned in Dreams. Fashion and Modernity*. London: Virago.

Winnicott, D. (1950) 'Some thoughts on the meaning of the word "democracy"', in *Home is Where We Start From*, Harmondsworth: Penguin, 1986, pp. 239–59.

—— (1951) 'Transitional objects and transitional phenomena', in *Through Paediatrics to Psycho-Analysis*, pp. 229–42. London: Hogarth, 1975.

Young, R.M. (1989) 'Transitional phenomena: production and consumption' in B. Richards, ed., 1989b pp. 57–72.

Zizek, S. (1991) *Looking Awry: An Introduction to Jacques Lacan Through Popular Culture*. Cambridge, Mass.: MIT Press.

NAME INDEX

SUBJECT INDEX

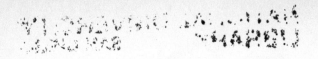